Pg. 64

Pg. 72 -- When you look upon something
which reflects the Light to you,
it is symbolic of the Light which
you are.

*Thank you, Jeshua, for always being here with us, re-minding us to pause, to choose again, to breathe ourselves Home into our Whole-Heart Selves. How wonderful to experience within ourselves the ever-filling, ever-flowing vibrational Love of our perfect Divine Selves, and to know in stillness and quietness the wisdom of God-thinking. Thank you for the awareness that we* are *the Kingdom of Heaven on Mother Earth.*

— The Reverend Marcia Bond, M.S., A.R.N.P., spiritual psychotherapist and long-time student of *A Course In Miracles*

Pg. 17 -

# Jeshua

# The Personal Christ

*Messages from*

*Jeshua ben Joseph (Jesus)*

*Volume I*

ISBN 1-878555-08-1

Published by
Oakbridge University Press
4007 Harbor Ridge Road N.E.
Tacoma, WA 98422
(253) 952-3285
E-mail: Judith@Oakbridge.org
www.Oakbridge.org

Second printing

Cover and interior design: Thomas Coates

For my mother and father,
who brought me up
in the way of the Lord,
and who have nurtured within me
openness of mind and love for all life.

Heartfelt thanks to all, seen and unseen,
who have assisted in the preparation
of this book.

A special thanks to Ed Mayer

# Contents

Beloved one,
          I come as your
                    Friend
because you have called me forth.


          I come as your
                    Personal Christ
until, awakening, you remember
          the One that we are.

# Preface

It has been my honor and privilege since the spring of 1993 to allow the very dynamic energy of Jeshua ben Joseph/Jesus to utilize "my" body to "be amongst the people" and to share His messages of love. The unfoldment of this process has brought up within me some reluctance ("You want me to do *what?*), many questionings, and much joy as I have seen His love received and lives healed.

Jeshua, through me, is the *personal* Christ, the One who enjoys reaching out and touching, gently messing up someone's hair, admiring a moustache, sharing a joke that reveals the Truth about someone. Times with Jeshua in this manner are very personal. They are times of laughter, times of tears. They are times of shared intimacy in the safety of unconditional Love.

The messages in this book are taken from transcripts of channelings given on Sunday mornings at the Oakbridge University Chapel or evening gatherings sponsored by the University. Jeshua's messages are always given in love, in simplicity, in humor, and with a good bit of down-to-earth practical wisdom. He is the Friend Who understands, Who supports, and Who offers the healing that comes with the holiness of Whole vision.

It is my hope that through the following pages you will enjoy an ever-expanding, ever-deepening friendship with The Personal Christ.

*Judith Coates*

Spring 1995

# Foreword

It is late afternoon. Jeshua and you are enjoying the coolness of the waning day. Rhythmic waves lap upon the shores of Lake Galilee and the gentle breezes move your strands of hair with caring delicacy. Jeshua turns to you, and like a tender brother, speaks words of loving instruction.

This is a scene which probably was enacted many times in a historically ancient time. Today, the same thing can happen to each of us, even though the circumstances may be different.

# Foreword

With fertile imagination, we can transport ourselves anywhere, pick up *Jeshua, The Personal Christ* and hear the Presence speak to us as he did to our sisters and brothers in an earlier century.

Suppose, in one of these intimate sessions, Jeshua asked you to identify the singularly most important question in your spiritual life. What would it be? After reading *Jeshua, The Personal Christ*, it became clear to me that the question is "How do I live in the Real world while living in the illusionary world?" Then, I had a second awakening. I realized that through reading this book, I was, at the same time, reading the answer to my question.

Read and meditated upon, this book can produce a cataclysmic experience for all that is limiting in our lives and a catalytic experience for the potential that our love can activate. Awakening by awakening the process takes place.

But no awakening comes easily. It involves stimulation, integration and expression. Of the three, the most difficult by far, and yet the most spiritually consequential, is expression, the fruit of total integration. Each new perception stems from the conviction that we are inseparable from God. There is never a moment in which God is not the Presence that we are.

Everything we do is an "act of Oneness." If this is difficult to understand, picture a glass of clear water. Mentally, pour food coloring into the water. Now, try to separate the water from the coloring. Impossible? Of course! It is equally as impossible to separate ourselves from God as it is to separate the water and the coloring.

Jeshua tells us in his book that, if we are convicted of our inseparableness from God, then the expression of this belief is visible in the choices we make. Through *Jeshua, The Personal*

*Christ,* we learn that the single most significant procreative act in our lives is the act of deliberate choice in each holy instant. The spiritual norm for choice is whatever is for our highest good or the highest good of others. How do we discern this highest good? Jeshua instructs us to choose what feels the lightest, that is, what is most filled with Light.

Not only are we the very energy of God, but we have the means to develop this energy to an infinitely exponential degree through choice. As our choices become more and more refined, informed by unconditional love, our energy vibrations increase in proportion. Then love becomes the very fire of our being and we accept it as the guide for our own expansion into greater and greater intensities of love as we make each choice from the knowledge of our highest good.

Jeshua walks with us through this book, speaking eloquently on many topics, but none with more passion than on the theme of love. He tells us that every circumstance, every person, every opportunity has its special face of love. Those who know themselves to be inseparable from Blessed Energy will recognize this special quality because love calls to love. In the most painful circumstances, that love cries out and we respond with deliberate choice to the highest expression of unconditional love.

Those who read this book will feel Jeshua's passion. Because of his love, we will never be satisfied with our love. It will always be growing, always be intensifying, until the tiny spark in our hearts becomes a torch whose eternal violet flame will be the sign of our everlasting love and a dazzling, pulsating Light that radiates throughout the cosmos, immersing in it every created being.

*Most Reverend Dr. Marilyn L. Sieg,*
*Bishop, Old Catholic Church, retired*

# Introduction

**B**eloved and holy and only Child of the Heavenly Father, Child of the one Source, Child of Light divine, I am the one known as Jeshua ben Joseph, — Jesus, you have called me — and it is in great joy that I come to abide with you now, as you have chosen to turn the focus of your attention unto me. I take the opportunity to speak with you through this, my ancient friend and teacher, the one known as Judith, because she allows me to speak through her. When I call her my ancient friend and teacher, this is true, for when we walked the Earth together, she was at one time my teacher in the Essene community where we lived. But when I call her my teacher that does not make her any more special than you, because you are also my teacher. We are all teachers one unto each other. Even now when you may perceive me as being ascended and being somewhere apart from you, I can go nowhere without you, for we are one together as our Father's holy creation. And though I show not a body identifiable as Jeshua ben Joseph and you see me not, I am with you always. You are the essence of me, as I am the essence of you.

You are my teacher, as I am your teacher, for the Mind of God is ever-expanding and ongoing, ever-experiencing Itself. The Mind of God is not static. It is dynamic. And as you experience, I experience; as we experience, the Totality, the Mind of God, experiences. Each seeming individuality serves the other one; each is the teacher of the other.

I come in this manner because of an alignment, an agreement which has been made. I come and I speak through this one even though she has reluctance to do this. She has resistance; she has feelings; she has doubts. She says to herself, "What is this all about?"

It is all about awakening. As you share in what is happening in this manner, she is awakening. And as you acknowledge the Awakening within her, know that it is also happening with you because you could not perceive it if it were not also true for you. Know that as you have chosen to read these words, to contemplate the ideas and concepts presented herein, to resonate in the heart with the Truth as it becomes remembered, you are awakening.

I have asked her to make this demonstration because many of the friends who have known her for some time have known the mouse that she has perceived herself to be — a mouse who is now finding her voice.

So, the demonstration which is now occurring is to show you that a mouse can find the courage to speak her truth even though she has her own doubts. The importance is for you to know that you can have the courage to speak your truth, to open the mind to new concepts and to allow the heart to come fully alive. You have come to a crossroads where you have had to make a choice, a choice of living in separation and limitation, a choice of merely living one day at a time or the choice to walk the path of the Father, of knowing that you are much more than what the voice of the world describes.

You have made the choice: the choice to walk the path of the Father, to live in your own Light, to express the joy which you are.

The time is now upon your plane when there is much need of the Love and the joy which you are to be shared with your fellow brothers and sisters. There is an acceleration of energy coming to this plane, an acceleration called forth not by masters apart from you but by the masters you are, and it will either be used in a positive way or in a negative outpicturing. The energies which you see show you many events where people are confused, feeling an intensity, feeling an onrush of energy and power, and a confusion: what do they do with the energy? Where do they go?

Your prisons are full to overflowing with people who are confused, who want to know their ChristSelf, who want to know Who they truly are. Your hospitals are full to overflowing with people who are confused and hurting because they want to know. In their soul they are crying out to know, "Who am I? Is this all there is?"

# Introduction

You are the ones who can share the vision with them. You are the ones who can shine your Light upon the situation and allow opportunity for seeing anew. You are the ones who can open a window and let in a bit of fresh air for them. This is your mission. It is what you have asked to do because it allows your awakening as well.

This is not the first turning of an age, as you would see time to be, which you have chosen to participate in. You have been here for other turnings of the age and have helped usher in other times of enlightenment. There is a knowing, an understanding however subtle, deep within your soul.

You have made the choice to call forth Heaven upon Earth. And I come because you have called me forth. I come as your servant. I come as your cheerleader. I come unto you to remind you of Who you are, of the Spirit which you are, and the dynamic quality of the Light which we are.

I come forth to be with you from the place which you and I share and have shared since before time was. I come to abide with you because I love that which you are. And that which you are is perfect Peace, perfect Love, perfect Light, Intelligence beyond your utmost imagination.

You are your Father's holy Child. You are my brother. You are my sister. I behold you as mySelf, the one Christ.

*Jeshua*

# Channeling

**M**any in your world have asked, "What is channeling?" And many have been afraid of it and have said, "Channeling is opening to things that I do not understand." And that statement is very true in the world: the ego sees much to fear because it does not understand, cannot comprehend the Whole Self. Channeling is opening to a greater awareness of Who you are. In the Dream of the Holy Child — which is Who you are — you drew an imaginary boundary, a boundary around the body and around the personality that you feel yourself to be, and have said, "This is all there is to me. This is who I am" — forgetting that you were the one who drew the boundary in the first place. You are the one defining the boundary. And in doing that, you have drawn a boundary in a great sea of beingness, the great sea of beingness which you are. That boundary exists nowhere except in your own mind and belief.

When you open yourself to a greater awareness, you are opening yourself to the rest of the sea of Light and Beingness. You go beyond the boundary for a moment or two when you sit in meditation and you feel an expanded sense of Self. You are going beyond the self-imposed boundary which you have put there, and you are tapping into the greater part of your Self. There is nothing outside of you. There is *nothing* outside of you. There is nothing to fear. Everything that you experience is in your consciousness and it is you.

So, therefore, when people in your world who have feared channeling say, "How can you believe in channeling? Why would you want to channel or to see someone channel? That is giving your power away to another being," know there is nothing outside of you. You, as you witness what is called channelling or allow yourself to "channel", are opening in awareness to your expanded, total Self. I am not separate from you. Even though I am speaking to you as what seems to be another individuality, I am not separate from you. My life is your life and your life is my life. You could not relate to, comprehend, empathize with my life if it were not within your consciousness as your Life. We are one. In channeling, what is happening, what is occurring, is an allowance into an expanded mind. It is an opening up of a greater awareness. It is an exchange similar to what is known in your scientific circles as osmosis, where there are molecules which pass through the membrane. This is what is happening in channeling. When you open yourself to a greater awareness, you get the molecules flowing through the membrane of the boundary that you think you have put around yourself.

You are not giving your power away. Quite the opposite is true, just the reverse is true: you are reconnecting with your power, even though you may at first identify it as being another individual energy. You are becoming aware of your greater Self.

Now, in Truth, there is no way that you can give your power away. You are the power. You can deny the power. You can deny the power of the total Self by saying that "I am only what is within this boundary," but all you do in that moment is to deny your power. You do not give it away. You cannot give it away. It is Who you are. You are the power.

So when others say to you, "What is channeling?," you can say to them, "It is tapping in to the greater Self that I am. It is sharing love and wisdom with other individuals which I perceive to be individual but who are not separate from me."

As you receive information via channeled methods, allow the same discernment you would use for information received via teachers, friends that you see utilizing the form of a body. Ask yourself, "Is this information in alignment with the Truth as I know it? Does it feel true to me? What is my knowingness?" Abiding in the Heart of yourself, in peace and silence, listen for the still, small Voice. Ask for the verification and understanding which comes from the perspective of Whole vision, holy vision.

Allow yourself to channel your Higher Self, as it would be called, for in willingness to contemplate, to dialogue, to channel more of your total Self, you awaken and remember the holy Child that you are.

You are beautiful. When I behold you, when I see you, I behold only your radiance. You have been told that you are an energy field, and this is true. You are a brilliant energy field which stretches out far beyond your imagination. You touch everyone else walking on this planet. You touch everyone else in the far universes. Think not that your life has small meaning. Think not that your life has no purpose. You are an expanded energy field and you are moving through the imaginary boundary which mankind/womankind has accepted for eons of time. When I look upon you, I see nothing but your radiance. You are beautiful.

Indeed, beloved one, you are a great ray of Light. You are Light and Love expressing in human form in the body, but you are much more than that. You are much more than the body that sits in the chair and much more than the personality with which you identify in this space and time.

Only a percentage of you is expressing at this point of focus, the personality in this space and time. Other percentages of you are expressing in other dimensions, other spaces and other times as well. Because you identify so closely with this focal point, you sometimes feel that this is all there is. But as you have experienced in the expanded consciousness of meditation, you can tune in to the other percentages of the whole and become aware of more of your total Self.

Play with communing with the other percentages of your-Self who are experiencing another dimension, another time, space, and see where they are. What are they doing? How are they feeling? Can you, in your love, talk with them and express love to them? Play with the idea of yourself in other dimensions and talk with yourself as you express in other times. There is no separation, except as what you would see in the temporary limitation of belief. The communion can happen at any time.

I come today to commune with you but I do not come alone. I cannot come alone for the Child of God is one, and wherever I am, I come with my brothers and sisters, those of Love and Light, and the room where you now find yourself, if you will receive it, is full of beings which you would know as friends and masters, guides and angels, full of Love and Light for you.

Blessed is your love and the love of others who are close to you, closer than breathing. I have come to speak with you now because you have called for me. I come anytime that you stop and pause and turn your consciousness and your attention unto me. And the same is true for the other masters and friends who are present in this room. Whenever you stop for a moment and call upon them, they are with you.

Those that you may have perceived as having laid down the body and gone on, have actually gone nowhere. They are here with you. If there is someone for whom you have felt a loss, someone who has gone from you, and you want to talk with them, know truly that they are still with you and that you can converse with them.

There is no expiration date beyond which you cannot make contact. If there is something you wish to express to a mother or a father or a loved one who has gone on, even years ago, they are still with you and you can commune with them. The same is true of ones that you have read about and have felt they were in your history, maybe a long time ago, and you wish you could have a conversation with them.

Beloved one, you can — the same as you are having a conversation with me. They are also present anytime you think of them and want to talk with them. No one is gone from you. There is nothing outside of you.

So if there is something that you wish you had expressed to someone and you feel that they are gone, turn in your meditation to them. Pour out your heart to them. Talk to them and then — just as important — listen, because it may be that they have a message for you. Pour out your heart, talk to them as if you could see them in body and then, listen. Because truly the Child of God is one and there is no separation.

There has been an evolution in the willingness of mankind to consider the possibility/probability/reality of the expanded awareness which I will call the Whole Mind of God. Books have been scribed, such as the little book that I authored around the turn of your past century called *The Impersonal Life* — you may be familiar with that book — and then closer to your time frame now, the *Course In Miracles*, another book which I have authored. I have been speaking through other channels, and there have been other, as you would perceive them, individualities who have expressed in channeled form, as the evolution of mankind has progressed, according to what mankind would accept in consciousness. At first the channeled beings seemed very much separate from the one who was lending the body, as in the case of the one known as Ramtha and the one known as Mafu, who have come through full-bodied, very much, seemingly, an individual personality.

Part of the evolution of the expansion of mankind's consciousness has been to understand that there could be a channel, a vehicle for information from what seemed to be another dimension. And as this has progressed, there has been a refinement in the channeling process itself, to the place now where you experience conscious channeling, conscious expansion.

The veil is becoming very, very thin. You no longer need to perceive the channeled energy as being something separate from you and something perhaps above you. You are willing now to know — and you are ready now to hear this — that I am one with you. You are experiencing an expansion, a releasing of limited belief of what Reality is.

Know that I am with you as you read these words. The veil which you have perceived to separate us is very, very thin. The evolution of willingness is coming to a place very rapidly now where you will be experiencing conscious communication with me and with other masters, with others who you feel have laid down the body and have gone on. This is part of the evolution of awareness of your total Self. It is something you have prayed for, you have asked for, and it is something that is now being manifest upon this plane.

Lo, I am with you always. When I said that, seemingly so long ago, I meant it literally. Beloved one, I am with you always.

Truly, the Child of God is one.

# Awakening In Every Moment

**B**eloved one, I would tender a suggestion to you, a suggestion that, if you will follow it, will transform the very life you lead: In each moment be fully aware of the Love that you are. Be very present with every thought that you think. Be very present with everything that you do.

For example, in this moment be present with the feeling of a smile, with the subtlety of how the eyebrows feel as they are moved, the tiny muscles which allow you to express inner delight or question. Be very present with how the larger muscles allow you to walk about and to reach out the hand unto someone: such a simple gesture and yet how much it conveys.

Verily, when I come in this manner, being amongst you with physical body, the joy of being present with you, being able to reach out and touch, is a joy which I share with you. When I pick up the beautiful, delicate strands of hair and feel them falling across the fingertips, I am reminded of the infinite variety of expression of the Love of the Heavenly Father. It is the Love incarnate which you are.

Truly nothing more need be done in this lifetime, if you will receive it, than to be the simplicity of Love itself. You need do nothing more in each day than to awaken and to smile: first at the light which you see with the physical eyes, and then to smile as the Light which you are and to extend that Light freely unto others you see in that day. Every day is a gift which you give unto yourself. It is an opportunity to be in conscious awareness of that which you already are: to be the song of the Heavenly Father, the song which is waiting to be sung so that your brothers and sisters may hear it and know that they have a song in their heart as well.

You are, if you will receive it, beloved angels walking upon our Holy Mother, the Earth. You are the Light come down, as it were, from Heaven. And yet, I say unto you: there is no coming down. You are the up. You are the down. You are the far and wide.

You have heard it spoken that this is the time of Awakening. There has been a cry from the soul of mankind to know Its

Truth and to awaken. And I say unto you that by being present in every moment you will find yourself to be awake. It is not something that is far off which needs to be awaited. It is not an event to be experienced only in your days to come. It is right here in every moment. Every moment as you lift up your eyes and you behold the beauty of a leaf upon the tree and the play of the sunshine upon the leaf, as you behold the way a flower opens to the sunshine, the way the songbird sings in the morning and at eventide, each time that you look upon your brother and sister and you behold the smile, the Christ Light, in them, you are truly awake. It is not something which you have to pray for, which you have to strive for, which you have to be good enough to experience. It is here every moment with you. It awaits only your choice to be present with whatever is in front of you and to behold it in holy vision.

If you will receive it, you are awake in this moment as you come unto that place of peace within the heart. This is Who you truly are, and you are awakened. Now, this is not to say that there will not be times that you will have other things upon the mind and you will go asleep within the Dream. But if you will remember to breathe with consciousness, being present with the breath, you bring yourself back to the place of peace and you bring yourself back to the Awakening. You are awake in every moment that you so choose, and as you would see these moments strung together without interruption, you will feel a power in the realization: the power of coming into remembering Who you are.

There will be cosmic laughter upon this plane as each Son and Daughter realizes that he/she has never strayed from the Kingdom, for the Kingdom has always been within. It is always with you. You cannot lose it. Verily, I have said the Kingdom of God is within. For it *is* you, when you remember the peace which you are and choose its expression as Love. It is a state of being, fully realized. Then you are truly awakened.

Awakening comes in grand simplicity. There does not need to be the fanfare of angels singing in your heavens and a great opening of the clouds, the heavenly host descending and saying that this one — or this one — has awakened. But there *will* be a joy which will be singing within your heart, and it will be as if the heavenly hosts are singing with you because you will feel such an exhilaration of Who you are.

There has never been the necessity to await awakening. There has never been the necessity of lifetimes of study in the monastery, books studied and exams passed to make you worthy of the Awakening.

You would ask, "Well, why have we accepted that it must be something to be accomplished? Why does it seem to be something outside of me?" It is because, beloved one, within the Adventure the Son of God/Daughter of God chose to say, "I will see what lies beyond my Father's Kingdom and I will experience all. I will be the great adventurer. I want to know all there is to experience. I want to know if there are any parameters to what the Son/Daughter of God can be and can experience." And so you set out upon a grand Journey to experience everything which the Mind could imagine.

And upon this very premise of believing that there must always be more to experience you have put the Awakening, the At-one-ment, the Atonement, outside of yourself and have seen it to be something to be accomplished. It has been part of the very premise of the Dream itself that there must be something more. And yet, I say unto you: you have carried the Kingdom with you wherever you have gone.

You have never left the Kingdom except momentarily when you have turned your attention unto other feelings and activities which you have felt were more real. And yet they have been part of the Dream.

Whenever you have stopped and you have taken a deep breath and come unto the place of silence where you could hear the still small Voice, you have awakened once more in the Kingdom. This is why I have said unto you that it is with simplicity, not with effort, that one comes unto the Kingdom. It takes only your willingness to accept the peace which you are.

From that peace everything else is added unto you. For when one abides in the peace of the Heart, attending only to the still, small Voice, all wisdom, all power is granted unto you. You are truly the Child of our Heavenly Father and there can be nothing denied you. There is nothing hidden from you. It takes only your willingness to come unto the place of the Heart, the place of peace, the Kingdom within, to ask and then to listen.

So often mankind will cry out unto me or unto our Father in sorrow and in confusion. "How do I get out of the situation that I see myself in? How do I become happy? How do I find fulfillment? How do I find love in my life?" And in the asking, there is so much confusion of energy that the answer cannot be heard.

Have you ever been so caught up in your emotions that you could hear nothing else except the turmoil within your own mind and body? Yes. It is something that everyone upon this plane has experienced.

Breathe. At times like that, remember to breathe, to be present with the breath. Such a simple thing, and yet it brings you back again unto your Self. There may be times when you will feel so much energy with the emotions that you need to run through them, as it would be, until they are spent. Allow the energy to be spent, beloved one, for on the other side of that expenditure there is a deep and abiding peace.

You do not need to feel that you will be lost in the emotions, for they will not consume you. Allow them to take their course; you are stronger than your creations. Allow them to be what they need to be, and you will find, on the other side of the expenditure of the emotions, your Self, the peace which you are. Then seize the opportunity to listen. Do not start to re-create what you have just been in, with all of the worries and all of the "what ifs." Abide in peace and listen.

Each day, as you go out into the sunshine which you have manifested, look with new eyes at the trees, at the flowers. Stop for one moment and take within the fingertips a tiny blade of grass and behold the miracle which is being its process just for you. Be very present with the blade of grass. Speak unto it. Ask it what it would share with you — and listen. There is peace in talking to a blade of grass and there is great healing in the simplicity of a blade of grass. It is there to share with you the joy of its process of Life.

Verily, each day is the day which the Lord hath made, for you have made it. Go and rejoice in it, and know yourself to be the Child of our Heavenly Father. And do you know how the natural child goes? With simplicity. Not wondering what the next hour is going to bring or what should be done or how anyone else is going to look upon what they are doing. A child is so immersed in what is happening at the moment, they are very much present with that moment and enjoying the blessings thereof.

Be the Child of your Heavenly Father. Be very present with everything and everyone, appreciating every nuance and subtlety. Be very present with each moment. Acknowledge the peace of the breath, and know that in that peace unfolds your remembrance of the Awakening.

# You Are Perfect

**D**early beloved, do you know how loved you are? You are your Father's only creation, created before time began. You are His holy Child, created whole, holy. You are eternally the joy of our Father. Sometimes in this world you have chosen to turn the focus of your attention unto activities and attitudes that the world would suggest to you, and you may have chosen to see yourself in another light — or lack of it — but at all times you are the Child of our Heavenly Father, created as perfection. Nothing you have ever done or have ever said or have ever thought will change Who you are.

Nothing others have ever done or thought or said to you or about you will change Who you are.

You are the Light, unlimited, unbounded, forever expressing. Would you judge the Light? Light does not judge itself. Light *is*. Light pours forth — and in pouring forth, scatters the darkness before it.

In this day and time of what you see as your world, there are many voices speaking unto you, many voices which would call you unto activities, schedules, to be so busy that you would forget the peace of the Heart. Sometimes you find yourself so caught up in the activities of what you feel must be done by a certain time that you forget to extend the Love which you are to others, to yourself, and even to the body which serves you so well. And yet, the simple process of taking one deep breath will restore unto you your center, your peace.

Breathe with me. Breathe in the golden white Light that you are. Take it deep within yourself and know it to be you. Feel it coming in not only through the mouth and the nostrils, but feel it coming in above your head, above the crown chakra, and take it deep within every cell of your body. Feel it energizing, flowing throughout the whole body, even to the toes and the fingertips. Whenever the world would call unto you and would speak to you of what needs to be done and would give to you a heaviness and a seriousness, remember to pause and to breathe.

For truly there is nothing you need do in this world except to remember your holiness — the wholeness which you are from before time began, the Child of our Heavenly Father — and to remember the holiness of your brothers and sisters, extending unto them the love which they are seeking, while yet a little while they know not that they are that which they seek.

For when you, in your courage, allow the Light which you are to shine forth in such radiance and such joy, you offer others the opportunity to see the Light which they are. They will catch a glimmer of a possibility. And, as you have experienced, joy is contagious. A smile spreads from one to another to another to another, and your joy is made manifest.

Your mission is not one of seriousness. It is not one of seeking. It is not one of purifying yourself. It is not one of sackcloth and ashes. Your mission is to be the joy of the Child of the Heavenly Father. And if others would speak unto you a different image, ask them why they would hold you in limitation or judge you when your Heavenly Father does not judge you, but only loves?

When others would come unto you with what is their truth and ask you to share their truth, be very present with them. Listen to what they are saying. Listen not only to the words which they are speaking to you, but also to what their heart is saying and what their heart is asking. Take what they are saying into your heart, and if it resonates with you, then you may smile and join with them. If it does not resonate with the Love and the joy that you know, if there is a constriction, smile also, and return it unto them. Say unto them that your Heavenly Father — which is theirs as well — loves you with an unconditional love and does not say that you need to be in a certain way in order to be worthy of His love. He loves you with the Love that you are.

So when ones would come unto you and would speak their truth unto you, you may smile and love them and allow them their path, even though they may not want to allow you, seemingly, your path. Smile and walk on.

You need not convince anyone of Who you are or Who they are. For truly the awakened Heart is one which will ask what you have found, for they will see joy and they will see peace, and they will wonder, "What has that one found?" And they will ask. But until they ask, your mission is only to be the Child which you are and to let those who have the eyes to see to behold the joy and peace, and then to ask you. You do not need to go abroad with great placards to convince others and win them to your side, as many in your world feel they must do. You need only abide within the Heart and to know that all healing comes from Love, from the wholeness which you are.

Your Father created you perfect. And if He created you perfect, you *are* perfect. Anytime there would come before you something which would speak otherwise, pause and breathe, and then ask, "Where does that thought come from? Does it come from the heart of Love? Does it come from the holiness that I am?" Or does it come from the separate self, the self that would speak to you of separation, that would speak to you of need to protect yourself, or need for action? Is it the voice of the world or is it the Voice of the Heart?

Everything in this week that you will manifest in your experience, test it by pausing for a moment and being very present with the thought, with the person, with the circumstance. Be very present with it and ask, "Where does this thought come from? Does it come from the world or does it come from the Heart of Love?" And then shine your Christ presence upon it, the Light of Who you are. For truly there is a Presence that goes before you. And it is not a presence of one that you would see outside of you, going before you to make the crooked places straight. It is your own Christ presence and your own Light that goes before you, *as you*, when you live in the awareness of Who you are.

We have spoken of living the Christed life. This is what you are desirous of experiencing moment by moment: of awakening in each moment of your day and saying, "I am the awakened Christ. How does the Christ look upon this situation? How does the Christ feel?" And if it seems afar removed from you in that moment, imagine how the Christ would feel, and put on the shoes and the raiment of the Christ and go about your day.

All healing of the body and of the emotions and of the circumstances that you see in your life, comes from the place of the Heart, the place of knowing that you are the Child of the Heavenly Father, our Father, and that as the Child of Light divine, having been created in perfection, you are perfect each moment. Speak that unto the very cells of the body. When they would feel weary, shine the Light of your Christ presence upon the very cells of the body. And I will share with you a secret: you will feel such an energizing that you will wonder if you have drunk something — and truly you have. You have drunk the elixir of the Christ Light which you are.

When there would be circumstances, relationships perhaps, in your life which do not seem as wholesome, as harmonious, as you would like to see, shine the Light of your Christ presence upon them and know that you and others are the Child of our Heavenly Father. You are one. What is it that gives you the life that you are? Where do you think we have come from? Did you just magically appear, like a mushroom overnight, upon this plane? You are the Child of our Heavenly Father and you are one with the Father. It is His Life that you are living. And if you are living the Life of our Heavenly Father — and I assure you that you are — you are perfect and you lack for nothing. If there is any circumstance, any aspect in your life that you would see changed, and if you truly desire, it will be changed.

It is wise to go first unto the Heart and to ask if something needs to be changed, for always there is more occurring than just what one sees upon the surface. There is much to be gained in going through what one would first see as a limitation — for you and for others who are watching. All of you are great Lights unto your brothers and sisters, though you know it not. The very peace and Love which you are speaks so loudly that you need not words.

So if there are circumstances, aspects that you would see changed in your life, go first unto the Heart, where all wisdom abides, and ask, "What are the benefits in this moment? How can I see this situation in the Light that it is?" And then if there is to be a change, you will know and you will also have the guidance to know how to make the change.

You are the divine Child of our Heavenly Father and you are all power, unlimited. You are all joy, which cannot be contained. In this moment, this very moment, return unto the place of the Heart. How does it feel to be the Child of the Heavenly Father, of the One that is as the King? How does it feel to be the child of a king? Do you lack for anything? Would not your Father give unto you that which you truly desire?

Abide within the Heart of all-encompassing Love, O Child of the King. You are His only begotten, created perfect from before time began. And when the purpose of time has been fulfilled, you will remain What you have always been: perfect, whole, holy, the divine expression of His Love.

# Reincarnation and
# Coming Home

M any of you have asked about reincarnation. What is it? Is it real? Reincarnation, beloved one, is where you would see yourself to be living and expressing through the different design patterns of physicality in what you call the different incarnations, the different bodies, expressing in different lifetimes in order to experience the infinite creativity of the holy Child.

You have been here as the grand warrior. You have played the part of the conqueror, and the conquered. You have been the grand master, and the slave. You have been the tyrant; you have been the lover. You have been the scholar who shared of the wisdom. You have written the great books and then have come back again to read those books and to revere the one who wrote them, not knowing that you were the very one who wrote them.

The holy Child desired to know, to experience the truly infinite expressions of Life, of creativity. The holy Child, abiding in the Kingdom of our Heavenly Father, asked of himself/herself, "What are the boundaries of this Kingdom? How far does it extend? What are the parameters? What is beyond this Kingdom? Is there a 'beyond'? What can I create?" And with those very questions all adventures, all journeys were begun.

This is the Dream, for truly, the holy Child has fallen asleep in the meadow of the Kingdom and dreams many dreams, many wonderful adventures, to experience Its infinite creativity.

Some of the dreams have been the dreams of love, the dreams of simplicity. Some of the dreams have been more as what you would call the nightmares. And there is nothing to be judged in any of these dreams, for it was truly your desire to experience all of the parameters. "How far does my creativity extend? What can I create?" And even in times of sorrow, times of violence, times of what you would say were negative experiences, that is a momentary judgment for you have chosen to experience what you would call the valleys, the depths, for you have said, "I choose to experience the depths so that I will know the heights when I am there."

You have chosen to experience all. You have chosen to experience the whole variety of life expressions, from the largest whale to the tiniest sparrow to the very rocks which make up the majestic mountains. You have been the king, the queen, the servant, the scholar, the one who is deaf and dumb but speaks from the Heart.

You have chosen to experience all to know your oneness with all. It has been for a grand purpose — not as a mistake, not as a judgment that would say that you had strayed far from the Kingdom, for truly you cannot stray from the Kingdom. The Kingdom is Who you are. The Kingdom is within. The Kingdom is you. You cannot be apart from the Kingdom.

But the holy Child in the journey, in the grand adventures, has felt himself/herself to have gone afar, for you would say, "Look at what I have experienced. Look at the journey I have been on. Look at all of the adventures. I must have come far from my Father's Kingdom." And in thinking that you are far from the Father's Kingdom, you think yourself to be separate from the Father and from His Love. And then the question arose, "What have I done to deserve the separation that I perceive? Surely I must have done something terrible. I don't know what it is. I don't remember what it is, but surely it must be something really terrible for my Father to have cast me out." But your Father has not cast you out.

You are always in the Kingdom. You are always as you were created to be. But the holy Child, thinking that he or she has gone on the journeys and has experienced so much, thinks himself/herself to be far away until you come unto the place where you now find yourself, the place of saying, "Wait a moment. Perhaps, just perhaps, all of my journeys have taken me in what I would see as a grand circle. Perhaps, I am coming Home again." And this is what you and your brothers and sisters are now experiencing.

In Truth, you have never left Home. But the Child, in the creativity which you are, has experienced many journeys, and even in what we talk about as coming Home, it is the process of belief that believes that there needs to be a coming Home, and yet, I share with you that you *are* Home already.

You, as the holy Child which you are, are creativity in expression. All of what you would see as the reincarnations are but as the grand adventures which you have chosen to experience for the fun of experiencing whatever you thought to create, and there is nothing of judgment in that.

There are many who would tell you that you have sinned and gone astray. Or that truly you have made a mistake in thinking yourself to be apart from the Heavenly Father. There is no mistake in it. There is only great creativity. It takes only for you to look one degree further to see that you are the one who is manifesting all of the journeys for the purpose of experiencing yourSelf.

Do you see what a gift you are to yourself? What a gift you have been in what you would see as all of the lifetimes? All of the experiences? For you have been as the one who amassed the golden coins and in one lifetime hoarded them, and took from others more and more and hoarded them. And you have come again in what you would see as another incarnation and you have inherited a great fortune of golden coins, and in that lifetime you extended them unto your brothers and sisters freely because you desired to experience what it felt like to extend.

There is no judgment. Your Heavenly Father does not judge you. Your Heavenly Father knows you to be Creativity, knows you to be the expression as His Child and awaits only for you to claim Who you are, to acknowledge It in Its fullness. That is what coming Home is all about. It is simplicity itself.

It is saying in one moment — the moment which you choose — "I am Home. I have never left. I only thought I had left. And I had a great time upon those journeys. I was the wonderful actor/actress. I played my parts with feeling. Each lifetime I experienced what I chose to experience." And even if it would be seen as suffering and times where you felt others were taking from you your very Life force — they cannot, but you felt that they were — you are experiencing your power, the power of creativity, the power of manifestation.

You are the master. It is only that you have held the belief that there needs to be a journey somehow to come Home. You are already Home. Home is where the Heart is. Have you heard that said in your world?

There is Truth in many of the sayings of your world. If you will abide with some of the sayings and take them to the very source of the meaning, there is Truth to be shared. Home *is* where the Heart is.

When you breathe — powerful simplicity — and you return again unto the place of stillness and you connect with the peace which you are, you are Home. It may be for an instant and then you may choose to again become embroiled in the drama you are creating. And there is nothing wrong with that choice. Let no one tell you that there is anything wrong with the drama which you are creating — except as you may want to change it to experience more joy.

If you choose to be in the confusion, in the activity of the world, and to listen only to the voice of the world, that is your choice and it is for what you would see as a time — which does not exist in Truth. And the final outcome will always be the same: you will awaken in one moment and there will be divine laughter, for you will know, "This is where *I* have always been. I am Home. I have always been Home. I am the Prodigal Son. I thought I journeyed unto a far land — and in my experiences I did, as the creative Child which I am." And yet, Home has always been where the Heart is. You can connect with it in any moment.

That is what is meant by walking the Dream in wakefulness: knowing that you are Home, that you are Home in the Heart, connecting with the peace which you are, the power which you are in that peace — not as the world defines power, for you do not have power over another individual drop of water in the ocean. But you have power, as the very being of Love which you are, to express Who you are, connecting with Home and then coming *from* Home in all activities, extending Love in every moment, connecting with the Wisdom which you are in every moment, being at home no matter where you would see the physical body to be. You are always at Home. It matters not whether you would be in the state which you call California or whether you would be in what you would see as a far country known as Tibet.

In the lifetime which I spent upon this plane, the lifetime which is so famous and well-known, I traveled unto many of the far countries. I traveled unto India. I traveled to Tibet. I studied with the masters. I traveled to what is now known as Great Britain and studied with the holy men there. It was provided for me that I could make these journeys, and I studied with ones who I thought at one moment were masters above me in wisdom. And as I studied with them, they shared with me that all wisdom is within, that the wisdom is not in what you would see as a teacher. The teacher can only be as a catalyst.

I come; I talk with you. I can be as a catalyst which says, "Remember Who you are. Play with Who you are." I can be as a sparkplug, but I cannot do it for you. You are a master the same as I.

When you look in the mirror, what do you see? You see a miracle of consciousness which attracts the very cells which form the delicate skin. You take it all for granted, and yet, each moment is a miracle of expression.

Reincarnation, beloved one, is the Grand Adventure of the holy Child experiencing all of the expressions of Life that you can imagine. It is a wonderful adventure, an adventure which in time allows the Prodigal Son/Daughter to acknowledge that you *are* Home.

# Passion

**B**eloved one, I come to join with you in joy — always in joy — because I come from the Mind of God. I abide within the Mind of God, a place of joy, the state of beingness which you share with me and have shared with me from before time began.

I desire to speak with you now about passion. You have heard ones speak of the passion of Christ, of my passion, and often this refers to the passion upon the cross and my suffering. This is not my message. This was not my truth upon the cross. I did not suffer. I knew that death and the laying down of the body is but one passage, one passage in eternity.

My passion is not the passion of suffering. My passion is not the passion of death. My passion is the passion of Life and for life.

Passion, my friend. Get some passion in your life. Be aware of the joy and the beauty in your life, and nurture the passion for living. Become alive with passion. Get into your life and love it — because you know what happens then? When you are truly one with the Spirit of life, you are consciously aware of the unlimited Love which you are, and you cannot wait to share your exuberance, your joy, with someone, whoever comes into your life at that moment.

Before you lay your head upon the pillow tonight and go to sleep, pick up the telephone and call someone, someone you may have had in mind, someone who has been coming to mind lately. Call them and share with them your joy. Share with them, "I've been thinking of you and I just got this nudge to call you and to share with you my appreciation." Share with them your appreciation of their friendship, their individuality, their unique expression of life. Share with them the beauty of this day, of the miracle of Life expressing as the lilies of the field, the song of the first bird of the morning, the unconditional love in the eye of the beloved pet or the small child. Your joy fills your cup and runneth over. Long enough has mankind/womankind focused on what is seemingly wrong or lacking in their life. Now is the time to shift that focus.

Those of you who have desired healing, know that in your passion is your healing. As you become truly alive and love your life, the small things of healing which need to be balanced in your body will be balanced. The body is an extension of your mind and of your thoughts. If your mind is at peace and in joy, the body will function perfectly. Live your passion and your healing will be true.

Become alive with **passion.** Become alive with the joy of the Father. Become enthusiastic; allow some *theos* —(God )— to be felt in your life. Be *en theos*. You are not limited. You are not held down by the personality, by the schedules which you feel you must keep, or by the "shoulds" of society. You are unlimited. You have experienced the resurrection.

You are already the arisen Christ.

Know this.

Express this.

Be this.

# The Energy That You Are

You are a great ray of Light. You are eternal; you are unbounded, forever extending and expanding the Love of our Heavenly Father. There is a dynamic energy in the molecules of physicality which you have chosen to use in the design pattern known as the body. When you come unto each other and you share with each other the handshake, the hug and the embrace, there is a true energy which is exchanged, which passes from one unto the other. Always your energy is in motion. The body does not contain the energy which you are; rather, your energy surrounds and activates the body.

pg. 37

35

# The Energy That You Are

Your brothers and sisters, when they come into your presence in a room, feel the energy that you are. This is why you may have walked into a room full of people and you may have felt at one with them and have felt a joy with them, an expansiveness, an at-home-ness, as you have called it. You have said, "I walked into that room and I felt at home" — because you recognized the Love energy which was there.

Sometimes you have walked into a room and it has felt strange for you because the energies which you perceived were not those that you identify with. It is all a matter of frequency. It is all a matter of expressing and allowing the Love energy which you are to be freely shared with others.

This is truly what you are coming unto now — a great freedom to express Who you are with joy, with love, with a dynamic energy which is alive in every cell of the body.

It is a wonderful time now that you are calling forth. It has been called a New Age but it is a remembrance of an old age — an age of enlightenment in which you remember the Light which you are. It is a time when you know that the veil which separates you from remembrance is very, very thin and is being dissolved momently within your consciousness.

It is an exciting time. Many lights are being turned on as you remember; many lights are being shared with your brothers and sisters so that they can know the Light as well. You do this in many small ways: in the light of the eyes, the light of the smile, the light and the love of just a simple word which is shared with someone, a word of encouragement, a word of insight which has come to you, part of your inner knowing, which you are then willing to share with others.

When I walked the Earth, so many years ago as you would see it, I had but one simple message to share with all of you.

## The Energy That You Are

My message was that I and my Father are one, and that you as my brothers and sisters, my equals, my friends in true nature, are also one with our Heavenly Father. It cannot be otherwise.

Many have come unto you with theologies, complex systems of religion, and have tried to explain in elaborate concepts and terms what God is, and have made Him a far off being, so complicated and so intricate that one could never reach Him. My Father and your Father dwells within your heart. My Father and your Father is Love — very simply. Your Father loves you with an everlasting Love which has been before time began and which extends beyond the boundaries of what you see as time. Your Father loves you with an everlasting Love because that is Who He is, and you, as His only creation, are that eternal Love.

Every morning when you awake and you become once again aware of the consciousness you are, the dynamic energy which runs through your veins, as it were, and activates every cell of the body, know that you are the Love of the Heavenly Father. You are the One expressing as the many. You are the sparklers on the Fourth of July; you are the sparkles which extend forever, expressing the essence of Love because you are that Love.

You have come to re-member, to put back together that which has seemed to be apart — remember — and in that process to remember for yourselves Who you are. To feel it.

For one does not come unto the Kingdom with words, but one comes unto the Kingdom with feeling, with the expression — which means the out-going, the ex-pressed — of Love.

Go first unto the Heart, unto the peace of the Heart. Sit with the peace in the Heart, until you can no longer sit with the peace because there is so much dynamic energy which has to be expressed. You will get up joyfully and will go unto your brother, your sister.

You need not worry about what to say or do. It is as simple as looking another in the eye and saying unto them, even silently, "You are the Christ that I am and in that Love I greet you." Nothing more need be done. And if the Holy Spirit — the activity of the Mind of God in Its Wholeness — nudges you to open the mouth and to speak words unto another, you will then be guided and you will know what words to speak. But if no words come unto you, know that you have spoken books, as it were, through the eyes.

It is a wonderful work which we do together, and yet, it is not work. It is joy. You are the energy of joy.

# The Energy of Your Name

**B**eloved one, I have felt your joy, albeit interspersed with doubts and questions from time to time. There has been a great level of energy you have been experiencing in recent months — a great expectancy.

Perhaps you would say it is because of events in your world. That is not wholly true. Perhaps you would say it is because of the people you encounter — and that is not wholly true. Perhaps you would say that it is for this reason or that reason. The reason is because you are the energy of the Father, the Child of the one creative Source, and you call forth everything you experience. When you open yourself to expressing and feeling the unlimited energy of joy, then you see outpictured for you what you call the reasons for the joy, for the expectancy, for the subtle hint of more to come.

And that is what I have come to address with you: the energy that you are, the creative, expressive energy. You have heard it said that you are a great ray of Light. And this is true. You are the energy of Light, experienced as Love.

But now we are going to talk about an aspect of energy in a different form. Many of you have been thinking in the past few months or even days of your time about your name. Many of you have been playing with the idea of changing your name. Many of you have been wondering what your name(s) may have been in other incarnations. It is not by accident that you have been considering names and their related tones. Names are vibrational energy.

Now, you may have come into this incarnation and have been given a name which you feel does not express your true nature. It may not express all of your true nature or you may feel that the sound thereof is not who you truly are. Or, you may have a name which you feel very much identified with, which feels like it expresses your true nature and Who you are.

When I walked the Earth some two thousand years ago in your timing, my name was a very powerful name. It was Yshwa. In the Greek form, it has been known as Jesus. In your anglicized form, it comes out as Jeshua, but in the day and time recorded in your holy Scriptures my name was Yshwa, expressing great energy, expressing an aspect of Totality in physical form.

All of you are a great ray of Light. All of you are giving yourself permission, at some level or another, to express Who you are and to share this with others. The time is now upon this plane when you are feeling more and more freedom to express

Who you are. So I would like you to take a moment, right now, to take the name which you have been given in this incarnation and to say it to yourself. Say it softly to yourself, but say it out loud. Abide with the gentleness and the nuances of the vibrations.

Now take that name and say it with great force as you would mean it, as you are calling unto the Heavens. Feel the power in the sound. Feel the expressive power of the vibrations.

Now, if you would like to play with an idea, play with a new sound — or combination of sounds — which may be coming to you, a new sound which you may feel is more of your nature. You may feel that the name you have been given has been incorrectly heard. Before you came to utilize the vehicle of the body all of you spoke unto your parents the name and the nature that you are. You whispered this unto them, and as they were open to hearing they heard the name and they gave that to you.

However, there were those of your parents who had an idea of what they wanted their child to be called, and even though you may have been whispering — or even shouting — unto them what your name and your nature and the expression thereof was, they may or may not have heard it or not heard it in its completeness.

You may choose what you want your name to be — how it would feel to you, how you would express the sound of the aspect of Totality which you are focusing upon in what you see as this lifetime. You are a great ray of Light. You are energy incarnate. You are a tone, a vibration, which is expressed in sound within the context of this plane of reality. Play with the idea of what your sound is, how it would be expressed. If you feel that the name which you have been given is too harsh, too short, too long, too soft, too whatever, choose what feels right for you.

This is something which you may then give unto the world if you feel that you want to, or it may be your own name which you keep just for yourself, your name which you use in the quiet time of your meditation.

If the name you have been given by your parents feels correct, agreeable, to you, you are Home already.

Play with the creative quality of your name. Add syllables; subtract syllables. Play with the vibrational expression. Speak it softly, caressingly. Speak it forcefully, with all the power of your being. Tone it over and over until you feel at one with the sound. As you do so, you will experience more of the unlimitedness of the expression of the holy Child which you are.

Be in joy.

# The Ego

**M**uch has been asked about the ego: what it is, why it is, what purpose it serves, how to overcome it, etc. Much has been spoken and written about how to understand the ego, how to come to terms with it, how to live with it or without it, all from the vantage point of the belief system of the one writing or speaking about it.

Ego, beloved one, has been part of the dream of forgetting. Ego is the voice of separation, which speaks that the holy Child, enamored of many adventures, has journeyed far from the Father's kingdom and is alone, separate, potentially vulnerable. It is part of the drama which you are saying you will play, part of the script agreed upon on this plane, the point of focus where you see yourself to be.

The ego is not known in other realities — realities with a small "r". The ego is very definitely not known in Reality — with a capital "R". But within the drama which you have said you will come and play right now, it is part of a belief that there is such a voice which would speak of separation. And yet what you are doing now is coming through that voice to a place of remembrance which says, "Oh, hey, this is just one of the plays of," — we will choose a playwright, such as Shakespeare — "This is one of the plays of Shakespeare. I've played with these plays. I've acted in this. I've done all of the roles which Shakespeare has written about. Now I will try another playwright." And then you go on to another drama which does not hold the belief in ego.

Ego has served you well in this drama. It has not been a mistake. It has been by divine choice. For you, as the holy Child, have chosen it as part of the ingredients of this drama. So it has been by divine choice, and you may thank it for the service it has given you. It has been your messenger, your teacher, pointing out limitation in belief, in image which you have held about yourself and your brother. Many, many times it has come and has knocked upon the door of your mind very strongly. Many times you have run very quickly when you have heard its message and you have acted in a habitual fashion, out of fear and belief in separation, out of judgment of self and others. But now, what you are witnessing — and allowing — is a change in response. When the voice of ego comes and knocks upon the door of your mind and insists that you let it in, you are now being rather discretionary about it, saying, "I think perhaps there is another way to look upon this situation." At that point, already you are calling in the expand-edness of whole vision.

Other times, in this lifetime and other lifetimes, you have not even paused to consider what voice this is. "Where does this voice come from?" You have not asked that question. You have heard the voice and out of fear you have been reactive — not proactive where you choose because you know you have choices — but you have reacted because you felt there was just one choice and you'd better get on with it quickly before something worse befall you.

Fear comes from the identification with form. It is form which can be threatened, seemingly, and yet even form cannot be threatened in Truth. For in the Resurrection, after I had allowed the body to cease its functioning upon the cross, I, because I knew my oneness with the Life force which we are, reactivated the body — reactivated it with the Light we are — and brought forth the form again, slightly altered in vibra-tional frequency. You do this also in a moment of happiness. You do this in a moment of revelation. Those who behold you as you experience a moment of great joy and revelation see a transformation even of your form. There is a heightened vi-brancy. It does not take what you would see as a tragic event of crucifixion to bring forth resurrection and transformation. You do that from moment to moment. Form awaits your direction; and yet, because of the increasingly intense identifi-cation with form, you have seen it to be your master and you have feared anything which would be seen as a threat to the form.

Now when the voice of ego comes up, thank it for being the companion you have asked it to be. Thank it for serving you in what you saw the drama of other lifetimes to be. But also you cannot deny that you now know that you have a choice, and the ego knows that you now know you have a choice.

So you see what has happened in this drama, this "improv," already? The ego must shift, and it does. Sometimes it gets a bit more subtle. Sometimes. But as you are vigilant within the heart, you recognize it and you say, "Stop. Stop a moment. Where is that voice coming from?" That is the question you need ask: "Where does that voice come from?" Then thank it for pointing out the possibility of limited judgment, and get on with the options, the choices to be proactive.

Ego has been seen as the great villain, something which must be slain. Much has been written about how to do battle with the ego, with the Tempter, with Satan, with evil. Well you know your battles with the voice of ego. When it has come and you have sliced off its head, it has then grown what you would see as a dozen other heads. Is this not true? It has come up in other ways. Allow yourself to be at peace with ego. Has it not been written, *Resist not evil*? When you resist, where does that keep your focus of attention? Where are you abiding in that moment?

The ego has served you well in the drama. It has been your messenger, your teacher, as you have asked it to be. You have asked it to be part of the script you have seen yourself playing. In any drama, there are certain elements of a script as it is presented, the "givens" of a drama. Then you proceed to improvise and you change from there on. But there are certain beginning elements, and that is what the ego has been: an element which you asked to be there.

Now you collectively are saying, "I am going to improvise and I am going to say, 'I have choices.' I have the choice to listen to the voice of ego which speaks of separation from the

Allness that I am, which speaks from a place of fear that says I must defend, that I must judge others, and that I must judge myself." But you have said, "No, I'm going to throw in a new element here. I have  choices. I have the choice to know that I am the One who has been scripting the drama."

And then everything, all of creation, shifts. So when the voice of ego comes up, thank it for being on your stage —for you asked it to be on your stage — and then choose anew. Choose a new script, for you are free to choose anew.

Choice is one of the other elements of improv which you have put into the drama. You are saying now, "I'm free to choose." And do you know what a great shift that has made in your drama?

And where did that idea come from? You. The great One which you are. One instant that idea wasn't there; the next instant it was there. You see the power of an idea. And everything shifts. So, thank the ego. Be at peace with it. Do not be at war with it. For as you have to be at war with something, you hold it tied to you in chains.

As you allow it to be only one of the elements in the script — and not a very important one any longer — it dissolves into the shadows in the wings somewhere offstage. Then you proceed with a point of focus which you choose. And that is powerful.

# If You Would Know
# Love in Your Life

**B**eloved one, I would share with you what would be called in times past a parable. Once upon a time — before time was — the holy Child of our beloved Father played in the Kingdom of His Father. And the holy Child of God — who is you — was very happy in the Kingdom and knew the joy of unlimitedness.

The Child of our Father asked, "How far does the Kingdom of my Father extend? What is within the Kingdom? What are the parameters of this Kingdom? What is beyond the Kingdom?" And with that thought, the possibility of all of the journeys and all of what you would see as lifetimes was born.

The Child became so immersed in and so mesmerized by his thoughts that it was as though he had fallen asleep and had forgotten that always he remains in his Father's Kingdom. With the very thought of, "Is there something beyond my Father's Kingdom?," all journeys were set in place. And, with the focus of attention stayed upon the journeys, having experienced seemingly many journeys, many lands, came the thought that, "I must have come far from the Kingdom. I must be far from my Father." And with that thought, the belief in separation was born.

Now, out of the thought of separation were established what you know as relationships, for as you would behold what you perceive to be another, immediately is established relationship.

Everything which you behold is a mirror for you. As you would look upon your flowers and your trees, upon the beloved pet, upon ones you would see as your brothers and sisters, there is immediately a relationship established, a relationship which mirrors back to you not only what you would regard as qualities of the other one, but mirrors back your image of yourself. As you look upon others of your brothers and your sisters, and you behold them, you behold yourself, for you could not acknowledge a quality in your brother if you did not have the computer program — the software — within yourself.

For, truly, what you see mirrors back to you your image of what you believe yourself to be and what you believe your world to be. If you would change your world, go unto the Heart, the place of perfect peace, and ask the one Teacher to allow you to see it anew, for truly, in each moment is given unto you the freedom to choose anew, to pause and to ask, "How can I see this in a new Light? How can I see this in another way?" And instantly there will be given unto you the wisdom of a perception which will bring to light a new way of looking at the situation, the person, the relationship. It awaits only your willingness.

When I spoke unto you to love one another as I have loved you, it was for you to know the Love which you are. And when I gave you the second commandment, to love others as yourself, it was for you to know that you must have love of Self in order to express this for others — even unto ones who would be coming and presenting unto you what you would perceive as the chaos and the tumult of life, the ones who are hurting and confused. Know that what is coming up for them are old wounds to be healed. For truly, all expression is either an extension of love or a call for love.

Many in your world would look unto relationships and to marriage for the fulfillment of needs, of aspects which they feel to be lacking, and they would look unto another to fill that seeming need. This is the reason why so many of your brothers and sisters go from relationship to relationship, always seeking another who will fulfill them. Know you that no other can fill a seeming need because there is not the need. You are whole and perfect as your Father created you to be. Your holiness is the wholeness which you already are.

If you would know healing, return again unto the place of the Heart, unto the place of peace. Breathe in the golden white Light which you are. Abide with me in the Heart and know the peace which you are. If you would know healing for the body, for the emotions, for relationships, for circumstances in your life, breathe in the golden white Light and abide with me in the Heart. There in that place of peace you will find all wisdom. You will find the answer to any question which may arise. You may be given guidance to move and to take action, to call someone on the telephone, to get into your chariot which has the horses inside and to travel unto another and to share your love with them. Or you may find you will be asked just to abide in the peace and to allow others their path.

If you would know love in your life, breathe in the golden white Light and take it deep within your Heart, abiding with love in silence and in peace. Feel yourself to be the beloved Child of our Holy Father. Know yourself to be within the Kingdom, for truly the Kingdom is you. You contain everything. There is nothing outside of you. You are the beloved Child of our Holy Father.

All choices which you have ever made have been used by the One I have termed the Grand Weaver, Who has used every choice and every twist and every turn, every manifestation which you have put in front of you, to weave the beautiful tapestry which brings the sleeping Child to wakefulness.

If you would know love in your life and in your world, breathe in the golden white Light. Take it deep within the Heart and, abiding within the Heart, feel yourself to be the unlimited Child of our beloved Father. Know that all others upon the path are you and they are the beloved Child of our Father as well.

If you would know love in your life and in your world, make the beloved Father your Lover. In every moment express your love unto your beloved Father, Who loves you with an everlasting love, with a love which will never be taken from you, will never be altered, will never be changed. If you would know love in your life and in your world, make the beloved Father your Lover, and you will be so filled with Love, you will not be able to contain it. You will not be able to hold it back. It will pour forth in its freedom upon everyone you meet, and you will know every relationship to contain the gift of salvation: to show you your wholeness, your *holiness*. You need ask nothing of the one in relationship with you, for you lack nothing. You are the Child of our Father, and every relationship is a holy relationship when you behold another as yourSelf.

Do not rush about in your world. It is not necessary. The world would speak unto you that there is much to be done, schedules to meet, places to be. And yet, the only place to *be* is in the Heart. Pause amid the voices of the world, and return unto the Heart, that place of perfect peace, and know Who you are. You express throughout eternity. You are the radiance of ten thousand daybreaks. You are the limitless Love of the Father.

If you would know love in your life, make the beloved Father your Lover, immerse yourself in the sea of Love which surrounds you, give the gift of your Love unto everyone you meet, acknowledging the Christ child which they are, and you will transform your world. It is time. You are the holy Child of our Father. You are the Love which you seek.

# The Face of Love

There are many faces, many expressions of Love. Love can be peaceful. Love can be exuberant. Love can be bubbling up from the depths within you and spilling forth. Love can be quiet, expressed through the eyes, through the smile, through the word which would support another, through the comfort of the arm about a shoulder, through a telephone call, a visit, thinking of another one and extending unto them what they may need at that moment.

Love can be, upon this plane, like the roller coaster. You may find someone who opens the shutters of your heart and ignites the flame, so to speak, within you, and you find yourself rising to the heights of emotion. And if that one does not then turn unto you and express to you the love you would seek, it can be as if you would be at the bottom of the roller coaster. And yet, what happens after that? There is again the upward climb. Hope springs eternal, and one is never left at the bottom. For as you would see yourself at the bottom, already the eyes are cast forth to the upward climb.

The roller coaster of love is the expression of love as your world has taught you: that it would be outside of yourself, something to seek, transitory.

The world would teach you that there are certain ways to expect love to come to you. The world would teach you that there are various packages of love which are more desirable than others. You see in your world a whole industry of the golden coins built upon the image of love and what it should look like and how to make oneself more attractive. And yet, beautiful soul, you are the Light of the Heavenly Father, always.

Love is Who you are. Love is the power which gave you birth as the great ray of Light which you are. You are energy. You are far more than what you see yourself to be in this time and space. You are a great ray of Light, energy ongoing, and it can be measured. Even your scientists in this day and time can measure that which you have called the aura. And you are more than that.

In the month which you dedicate to the celebration of Love, the month you now call "February," you send unto other ones the cards known as valentines. Why do you send unto your brothers and sisters the valentines? Why do you pause to celebrate Love, to celebrate, even unknowingly, yourSelf? It is because, at a very deep level, the soul desires to remember the Face of Love, to behold Itself in the mirror of Who It is. And as you send a message of love unto another, you afford yourself the opportunity to connect with that one, to come unto a deep understanding of oneness, feeling a desire to extend, to "reach out and touch" in some way. And as you extend, you experience Who you are. This is why I have said so many times unto you to extend the Love unto whoever would be in front of you. For it is not by accident that someone is in front of you. You have called them forth, as you call me forth. All of those you would see as your brothers and sisters do not just randomly appear before you. You have called them forth.

They are your messengers, and the ones you would send valentines to are your messengers — and your mirrors — as well. They are there as your servant so that you can extend unto them Who you are, so that you can feel the emotion known as Love, so that you can feel the energy in motion. Not static energy, but the energy in motion with the opening of the Heart, with the releasing of constricting perceptions about who you have thought yourself to be, about who you have thought your brothers and sisters to be, and about what you have thought the world to be.

In your days to come — and yet, they are already here — you will be seeing more examples of the face of Love in what you would know as your politics. You will be seeing a polarity which will bring about a clarity in awareness of whether one is abiding in the heart or whether one is abiding in fear and in the power of the world.

You will see ones in politics who will pause and will ask, "What am I doing and why am I doing it?" This is a time of evaluation for many. It will be a time of evaluation for countries in conflict, countries which have given themselves such conflict that many within the country will stop and re-evaluate, having to reassess what is going on. It does not have to come to such a dramatic point before the assessment is made, but oftentimes mankind calls forth much drama before it says, "Stop, already. Enough."

You will see this happening upon what you call your world front. You will see this in your health fields, as well. You will see the face of Love coming again unto the health and healing professions, where there will be advancements made in what is known as the conventional medicine not just for the golden coins but because there is the true desire to benefit ones of the brothers and sisters who are suffering. But even more so there will be the advances, as you will see them, in alternative methods of healing, where ones will want to find what will help others, not only of the physical body — that is true — but methods of healing the emotions, the baggage which has been carried for what would be seen as lifetimes. And the face of Love will show itself in the healing of body, mind and remembrance of Spirit.

There is a growing awareness that things cannot continue along the avenue they have been progressing without much pain and suffering, and that suffering does not need to be. More and more of your brothers and sisters will be choosing to abide in the Heart, to come from the place of the Heart, the place of Love, the place of saying, "I sit in the chair of my brother. I am one with my brother. How does it feel to be my brother? If I were feeling as my brother feels, what would bring me comfort?" And with that you will see the face of Love.

You will see the face of Love coming in technology, for as ones in the healing professions have ideas which will benefit, they will ask of the ones who can put this into your technological boxes, "How can we design something that will be more precise in measuring, more instant in healing?" And this will come about.

You will see the very programs upon the square box that you love to watch — not all of you, but many — you will see the programs themselves shifting unto a place where they are evaluating and asking, "What is important in life?" They will do this because there has been a cry from one such as you, a consciousness which is saying, "It is time for a shift in perception. It is time for more Love," very simply put.

And the ones who are into amassing the golden coins because you buy their products listen to what you say and what you desire, and when the consciousness of mankind and womankind shifts, as it is now shifting, the ones who are desirous of your golden coins will also shift. For as you allow a shift in perception to happen within you, all of creation will rearrange itself for you.

Mankind often feels that what changes, what is seen to change, is outside of him. Change happens, but it happens first within — and then you see the effects, seemingly outside of yourself. And yet you are the one who has put it into motion. The emotion of Love, the power of Love, the energy of Love, the energy of Who you are, is powerful.

You will see the face of Love in your neighborhoods more than you have seen. There is a growing wave of ones taking back responsibility for their neighborhoods and saying that, "We are a community and we must communicate with ourselves. We are responsible for our family, our extended family, for the community of the neighborhood." And you will see the face of Love again in the neighborhoods.

You have already seen the signs of the change, of many who are saying that there has been too much crime, too much violence, too many brothers against brothers. "Why," they are asking, "is this happening?" And they are coming unto the awareness that the acts of violence have their basis in the belief in separation, that, "I can do harm unto you and it will touch me not." Now more and more of your brothers and sisters are acknowledging that it is necessary to be together in Love, to express Love to the ones who are feeling that they must cry out so greatly with violence and with crime to get the attention, to get the love which they are asking for. Ones are seeing that love, if it is freely given, does not have to be demanded.

You will see the face of Love being extended in the neighborhoods and in the schools. And where does it come from? Where does the face of Love come from? From ones such as you who desire to know Love and live in harmony.

There is a wonderful wave which is sweeping across the face of this, our Holy Mother, the Earth. You have felt the acceleration in the last few years of your timing, especially in the last months of your timing. You will see the wave accelerating even more in what you call the days to come, and I would share with you it is not that they are going to come; they are already here.

For as you can cast your mind forward into the future and imagine what the future will be, I would ask you where that future is. It is right here and right now, in your mind. So it is not the days to come, although upon this plane there seems to be a process of time. There is a wonderful wave and you are part of it, a wave which desires to know and to see outpictured the Love you are, and to have your brothers and sisters also know the Love they are, to experience in fullness in the Heart Who they are. And you are the ones who are going to make that possible.

# The Face of Love

You are the ones who have already chosen to experience the holy Child, which you are. You are the ones who will say unto your brothers and sisters the word, the paragraph which they will need to hear. And it is not that you will feel yourself to be a scholar or one who will be a lecturer or one who is the master of ancient wisdom — although you are — it will just come forth from the Heart in the moment when it is needed. It will come forth in simplicity and be what that one needs to hear at that moment. And you may think nothing of it, but it will mean everything to the one who receives it.

Many of your brothers and sisters are crying out to know Love. They are crying out from their belief that there is no hope, no love, that no one will show them some hope, some love. You see this every day. They are crying out to know what you have at least accepted within the mind — and I would share with you that you have accepted it at the Heart level as well. Many will come unto you sorrowful and confused, with varying degrees of hopelessness and anger, and they are all crying out for one thing: the same thing which you have cried out for in times past — and perhaps not that long ago — to know, "Who am I? Why am I here?" Have you ever asked that?

You are here to share Who you are with Who you are. For truly, you never look upon a stranger. You look upon yourself. And you are here to share your Love in acknowledgment with others who still have what would be seen as the sunshades, the sunglasses, upon the eyes and do not see the Light which they are. You are sharing the Love and the Light with them. You will say unto them, "Lift up the sunglasses just a bit and behold the Light that you are."

You will do this in words. You will do this with a comforting arm around the shoulder, either literally or figuratively.

You will do this in your meditations, holding your brother/sister in the mind's eye of your Heart. You will find ways, because of your creativity, to share with them that which will heal. You will find avenues which will provide for them what they will see as the next step in their healing. And in doing so, you will be showing them the face of Love.

Every one you come in contact with every day, you show unto them the face of Love as you abide in the Heart, in Love, in peace, in song. For truly, all of you are a song which you sing unto your brothers and sisters — sometimes with more harmony than other times. Sometimes you would feel the notes to be a bit discordant within yourself and you would say, "I'm in a bad mood today." But know you, that can be changed in an instant, and you have discovered that you do not stay within what you call the bad mood as long as you used to; you have discovered that you have the choice of throwing it over the shoulder and saying, "What the heck. I've experienced that already. Let's try a new tune."

Many come unto you as servants of the Heavenly Father to show you avenues where you can serve, seemingly, and yet, what happens is that as you open your heart and extend the Love which you are unto ones — whether or not you feel there is something physical you can offer them, something in an action, something in tangible form — there is a feeling of support. That is the first step. And from that step come the other forms which you see within the world which will be helpful.

All of you, in the work which you do, are servants of the Heavenly Father, even if it is in something you would see as a routine task. For each time you allow the shutters of your heart to open, each time you connect with another one, you offer unto that one the opportunity to know their oneness as well.

Every time you are outrageous enough to say, "I see what you are talking about, but I see a grander vision. I know that you are the holy Child of our Heavenly Father the same as I am, and I know that we are unlimited" — you may not put it in those words; you will choose words which can be understood and accepted — every time you speak of the whole vision, the unlimitedness of possibilities, you allow them to know that there is at least a door they can walk through. They may not choose to walk through the door, but at least they will know that there *is* a door there. And whether they walk through that door in what you would see as this lifetime or several lifetimes down the road, that is their choice. But you have at least allowed them to know that there is a door, that there is something more than just the experience of right now, as you would see this body and this personality expressing.

You have allowed them to see past what they are experiencing at the moment and to put it into a little different perspective, as much as they will accept. That again is the face of Love: being outrageous enough to be a Teacher of God, to express Who you are with a freedom which says, "This is Who I am. This is Who you are, if you will accept it," and then to walk on.

All of you are great seed planters. You cast seeds as you go about. Sometimes they will be the seeds of doubt. You have done this in many lifetimes. The seeds of sorrow, the seeds of violence. But many times they are the seeds of love. And whether they fall upon the stony ground or whether they fall upon the fertile soil is not up to you. They will grow in their own timing and as the choice is made. It is only for you to be as the one who is the gardener and cast the seeds of love. That again is the face of Love: being willing to cast the seeds of Love and being willing to allow the seeds to do whatever they need to do.

There may be a tug at the heart which will want to see the seeds grow, and yet, neither you nor I can make those seeds grow. It is up to the choice of what would seemingly be that individual. And the One Who I have called the Grand Weaver weaves all of the choices together into a wonderful tapestry. It is only for you to cast the seeds and to be the face of Love.

# Meditation

I would do with you what is called a meditation, a meditation on the face of Love. Find yourself comfortable in your chair, and take a deep breath, breathing in the golden white Light that you are. Breathe it in deeply into the very cells of the body. Breathe in the golden white Light that you are and take it deeply within. Feel it lighting up every cell in the body.

Feel the golden white Light radiating at the base of the spine, the area known as the root chakra. See the Light as a root, connecting you to our Holy Mother, the Earth, anchoring your Light in this dimension, as you have agreed to do.

Feel the chakra of the solar plexus alive with Light. Breathe in the golden white Light that you are into the solar plexus, and see it expanding as the Light that you are.

And as you exhale, exhale the Love which you are.

Breathe in the golden white Light that you are and take it deeply within the cells of the body. Take it to what is known as the heart chakra and feel the Light of the heart chakra expanding. Breathe in the golden white Light that you are and feel it expanding the heart. See the heart glowing with the Light that you are.

Breathe in the golden white Light that you are and take it deeply within the cells of the body. Feel it expanding the throat chakra. See the Light expanding the throat chakra. Feel it relaxing and expanding, glowing with the Light that you are.

Breathe in the golden white Light which you are and take it deeply within the cells of the body, and feel the area of the third eye to expand. See the Light expanding in the forehead in the area of what has been called the third eye. Feel the Light which you are glowing, expanding, radiating.

Breathe in the golden white Light which you are. Take it deeply within every cell of the body. Breathe in the golden white Light which you are and feel it expanding the crown chakra. See the Light expanding at the crown. Feel it radiating. Feel it pulsating. Feel it expanding and releasing. Feel yourself to be one with the golden white Light which you are.

Breathe in the golden white Light which you are and take it deeply within every cell of the body. Allow it to be felt in the fingertips and in the toes. Allow the very fingers themselves to come alive with Light, the hands to be Light, the feet to be Light. Know yourself to be Light.

Breathe in the golden white Light which you are and exhale the Love which you are. And abiding in the stillness of the Heart, speak unto yourself your name. Take your name and call yourself as your Heavenly Father would speak unto you. Call yourself as you have heard me call you.

Speak unto yourself your name, with Love, with the Love of the Heavenly Father. Our Father. I and the Father are one. This is the Truth of your being. Say your name to yourself as your Heavenly Father calls you. Give unto yourself the Love which you have sought for so long.

Know yourself to be the Child, the holy Child of Love, lacking for nothing. Unlimited. All power. All Love. Worthy of that Love, for you are your Father's only creation.

Speak unto yourself your name as your Heavenly Father calls you, as you know I call you. Abide with that Love. Feel it to expand and to fill your whole being.

Breathe in the Love which you are. Breathe in your name and exhale Love. Feel yourself to be in the flow of the very energy of Love. For this is the Truth of your being. You are loved with an everlasting Love, for you are that Love. You can never be without it. It is your divine birthright.

You are the Child of Light divine. You are the Child of Love. Speak unto yourself your name as your Heavenly Father calls you. Hold the Child which you are in the everlasting arms of Love, for that is where you abide always. You are the Child, the innocent, holy, untouched, untarnished, beautiful, radiant Child of our Heavenly Father.

Breathe in the golden white Light which you are and take it deeply within the cells of the body. If you have been desiring healing, know that it has been accomplished.

Breathe in your healing. Breathe in the golden white Light, the golden white Light which expands and releases all illusion, all constriction; releases and loosens and lets it go.

You are the Beloved of our Heavenly Father, created before time was. You are a Child of Light: divine, whole, holy, eternal, ever ongoing. You are a vibration, a tone, energy. You are alive with the power of Love. Call unto yourself your name and know that you are loved as the holy Child you are. You have never sinned and you have never gone astray. All of the choices you have made have brought you unto this place of awakening. They have served you well. Everything has been your creation as the holy Child, the extension of the One Creator.

Breathe in the golden white Light which you are and take it deeply within the cells of the body. Send it unto any part of the body which would be calling out for more Light. Know yourself to be one with the Light and with any part of the body which would be asking for its wholeness.

If there would be healing of relationship, if there would be healing of circumstances, if there would be healing of the questions which come to the mind, if there would be healing of employment, healing in the awareness of the flow of the golden coins, breathe into those circumstances, relationships, the golden white Light which you are. Surround and blend the Light with whatever you would see to be needing healing, to be needing an answer, to be needing guidance, wisdom, wholing, holy vision.

Breathe in the golden white Light into whatever would be troubling, and allow it to speak to you. Everything you manifest in your experience is there as a messenger for you, as your servant.

Breathe in the golden white Light and take it deeply within the body. See it radiating and illuminating every cell of the body. See it expanding far beyond the confines of the body. See it blending into what would be the energy of your brothers and sisters. Feel the very vibration of the energy of your brother and sister. Know that your Light is one with your brother/sister.

## The Face of Love

Speak unto your brother/sister the message of your heart. What is your heart's desire? And listen. Receive the message of their heart. Thank them for being in your life, for truly you serve each other.

Breathe in the golden white Light which you are and take it deeply within the very cells of the body. Wiggle about the muscles of the body. Release them. Let them feel free. Feel yourself to be fluid, light.

Breathe deeply. Do you feel the peace which has descended? Do you feel the Love? It is not I who has brought this. It is you — you, by your willingness to return again unto the place of the Heart, to experience again the Love which you are, to come face to face with Love.

# Appreciation

Child of our Father, I would speak with you of appreciation. For when one awakens and knows oneself to be the Child of the Heavenly Father, one lives in appreciation, and humility and joy and exhilaration. For truly you are unlimited. You are unbounded. You are the joy which expresses forever and reaches beyond the farthest universes.

You are the energy of Light, expressing within this dimension as light coming through a prism. You express, seemingly, the various colors of light as individuality, and yet you are one great ray of Light, experienced as Love.

For it is truly when you connect with the feeling of love that you know Who you are. It is one thing for me to say unto you that you are Light — for this is what you are — but for you to know for yourself, you must go to the feeling, and the feeling is love.

When you are in a state of extending love unto another one, you will feel the heart open, the shutters will be thrown wide, and you will feel an expansion which is your true Self. Each time you look upon a beautiful painting, when you look upon the dawn and you are one with the angel of sun, each time you behold the newness of a puppy, of a kitten, any time you look upon an infant, a young child, a friend, and you see the smile in their eyes, you will feel the shutters of the heart open wide and you experience yourSelf.

My message is, and has been always, one of grand simplicity. It takes no great rituals, no lifetimes of study. It takes only the willingness to look into the eyes of your brother and sister and to behold the Christ in them. For when you behold the Christ in another, you behold the Christ which you are. There is nothing you will behold that is outside of you. Everything which you behold is you, for it is within your consciousness.

When you look upon your creations, the beauty which you have manifested in your world, know that you have put it there to remind you of the beauty you are. When you look upon something which reflects the light to you, it is symbolic of the Light which you are. When you look upon something which reflects the beauty, and you see it as a process which grows — it comes as a tiny bud and it opens into its fullness to share with you its process and its beauty — know that you have put that on your path for yourself so that you will remember your process and your beauty.

# Appreciation

Mankind has put *seemingly* all of the symbols and remembrances outside of himself to remind him of Who he is. You would look upon another and you would enjoy their beauty, you would admire qualities which you see within them — the quality of gentleness, the quality of wisdom, the quality of compassion, the quality of strength — and you would feel that they have developed those qualities perhaps more than you have, or you might even say that they have the qualities which you feel yourself to be lacking, I say unto you: you could not behold these qualities in another if you were not already that quality yourself. You are not separate from anything which you behold.

I would ask you to think upon ones who have been in this lifetime as friends, companions, ones you would appreciate for having been upon your path. Just cast your mind backward, as it seems, into what you call your past and number for yourself the ones who have been helpful, who have perhaps made a change in your direction, one who has shared with you something which has made a difference in your life.

Think of the quality which they have shared with you. Think of what they have represented to you. And say unto these ones "Thank you" for what they have shared with you upon the path. It may be a parent, a grandparent, a brother, a sister, a teacher, a friend, someone who has been there at the moment when you needed a word, a hug, an insight, and they have shared with you of themselves.

Perhaps it would be one who you would see as having been in another time frame, one who has written a book which you have read which has changed your life, has changed your way of looking at things. Speak unto this one, even though you might feel that they were afar off. You can speak unto this one and thank them for what they have shared with you. Behold the love which they are and which they have shared with you.

Speak unto the ones you have held in your mind and in your heart, speak unto them your appreciation for what they have shared with you — and then listen. What would they share with you? For truly there is opportunity for dialogue.

Take a moment now and think of when you have shared with someone and you have seen visibly that what you have shared with them has made a change in their life, a change in that moment. Perhaps it has been a friend who has come unto you in great confusion, one who was hurting, one who did not know what direction to go in, one who needed the peace which you are and to be reminded of the peace which they are.

See yourself as the giver of the gift that that one needed and that that one was allowing himself/herself to receive. Thank this one for receiving. For, you see, as one receives, one has given another the opportunity to *give*. And thank yourself for being the giver.

Give unto yourself the appreciation which you would extend unto others. Your world would say unto you that to give yourself appreciation is to be boastful and arrogant. And yet I say unto you, appreciate yourself as the Child of our Heavenly Father. Know your true worth, and then you can appreciate the Truth of your brother's worth. Hold yourself in limited self-image and you will see your brother in limited vision.

Would you give the gift of holy vision? Be vigilant in your appreciation. Abide in appreciation. Shine the light of your countenance upon that which is uplifting, inspiring. You are worthy to know yourself and the Truth of your being, and to live it with a light heart. You are your Father's holy Child.

# Purpose

**M**any of you have asked, "What is my purpose? Why am I here? Is it only to share a wee bit of happiness, to get through life with a minimum of hardships and to, hopefully, die peacefully at the end of it all? Is it merely to fulfill what society tells me I must do as I go through the various stages of life? Is there more?" And you have felt at a soul level that there must be more.

"What is my purpose?" Those of you who have a belief in reincarnation and have begun to claim your other lives, have thought, "Well, if I have lived many other lives, why am I here once again?" Know that your purpose is to awaken to the

Totality of Who you are, to integrate, as you would see them, the various lifetimes, qualities, aspects of yourSelf, and to awaken and know yourself to be infinite Creativity Which has thought Itself to be upon a multitude of adventures.

Your purpose is expressed and is manifest through being the Love which you are. That is why I have said unto you that relationship is your salvation — your relationship with others — because it brings forth from you what you need to look at within yourself which may be as blocks to knowing the total Love that you are. In every relationship be vigilant. Be aware of how you are feeling in that relationship. What is it bringing up for you?

When you are aware of what you may feel as a limitation, something which is not the total peace and the total joy and the total Love of the whole Mind of God, look at that part and abide with it because it is an aspect of what you have believed about yourself.

You are already perfect. You are already the holy Child of God. You are already whole. There is nothing you need to do to make yourself more perfect. Could you improve upon the creation of our Father? Your purpose is to remember His creation, to honor yourSelf and the ChristSelf of others, and to acknowledge Who you are with every choice.

In that acknowledgement, everything becomes a choice. You choose what you experience. You choose how you experience. You choose what you want your life to be. Not the constrictions of details, but the perceptions, that then alter even the specifics. How do you know what you are choosing? Look at what is in your life. This will tell you what you are choosing and, if it is not as you want it to be, you can choose anew.

# Purpose

When one knows that one is the Child of our Father, the happy, whole, loving Child of God, there is everything you can do —and yet the simplicity is that you do not have to do anything. You do not have to make it happen. You cannot of your own will make it happen, but you can allow it to happen through you — through the love which you share with others, through the expanded perceptions of how you look upon everything.

When you see a new puppy, when you see a new kitten, what do you feel inside of you? What goes out from you? How do you feel? The love which goes out from you can in any moment be expressed to anyone in any circumstance. This is Who you truly are — that feeling of Love. You have caught a glimpse of it. Live with that glimpse more and more.

The journey to God is a journey without distance. It is one of reawakening to where you always have been and to what you always are. The journey to God is one of awakening to know that you have not gone from the Father. You are the Child who has fallen asleep in the meadow, dreaming that he/she is far from the Father's Kingdom, yet all the while within you — *within you* — is the Kingdom. You are your Father's Child. You are Love activating the molecules of dust, known as a body, thinking perhaps that you are asleep.

Beloved one, I share with you now, you are awake. How does it feel to be awake? That is for you to tell me. Pause with me now for a moment. Imagine, *imagine* how it feels to know you are totally loved, that you are honored, that you are unlimited, unbounded, eternal, forever ongoing. Abide in the feeling of aliveness, exhilaration, joy. Know you can express and manifest your deepest desire. Know that you are your Father's holy Child right now — right *now*. Come Home with me. Say, "I am awake. I know Who I am." And as you acknowledge that choice, as you have the confidence and the willingness to acknowledge Who you are, your remembrance grows. You have seen yourself as a seeker. Know that you have found.

I do not come to share intricate techniques and rituals with you. Those are the playthings of the mind. You have initiated, formulated, perfected every technique and ritual in what you would see as countless lifetimes. You have been the grand author of ceremony who has returned in another lifetime to revere the ancient ones' wisdom in creating that very ceremony, the ceremony which you initiated.

I come to share the simplicity of the Heart, the simplicity of the knowledge that you are already awake and all it takes is your willingness to acknowledge, claim and *live* the Dream in wakefulness. I invite you to try that on for size as you would try on a new suit, a new coat. Try on a new wakefulness in your mornings — "I am the awakened Child of God" — and see how your day unfolds.

Beloved one, you are beautiful. Your radiance far outshines ten thousand suns. Go forth this day and remember your Purpose. You are the awakened Child of your Father, in Whom He is well pleased.

# Jeshua Speaks About Community

There is coming now a time of readiness for the vision which many of you have seen of a community. Many of you have held the desire of communion, of Family reunited, within your hearts, and it is already manifesting. What you are seeing in many of your gatherings, gatherings where there is support for one another, sharings from the Heart, is a community: a communion of the energy and a coming together in joy.

That is truly the essence of community. It matters not whether you are physically living in the same geographical location and sharing, as you would know, the bathroom, with each other. What matters is the communion of love from heart to heart, the sharing of one's self freely.

# Community

But there will be physical locations of communities which you are going to be instrumental in setting up and developing, and the time is coming when it will be appropriate to find physical locations.

Each community will be a healing community in the broadest sense of healing because there will be much joy in it. Much healing will be done through the sharing of the Love you are with others. Others will feel the acceptance, the unconditional love, as they walk upon the grounds and come within the energy field which you are providing there. It will be charged — and yet the charge for one staying there will be minimal.

I wish to share with you now a broad vision of what the communities will be serving. Each community will be a place, as you have envisioned, of great beauty, a place very much in tune with your Holy Mother, the Earth, a place in nature with the green of the trees, the green of the fields, and the healing power of flowing water.

There will be much peace upon this land. Already there is much peace there, and there will be a peace which you will bring unto it. Each community will be a place where some of you will be called unto to live. You will physically take yourself and your belongings and move unto that place because you wish to be there. There are others of you who will stay in the location where you are now, doing the work where you are needed now. But you will travel to a community from time to time to offer your services there.

Many of what you would see as the general population will come unto the various communities and spend some time, either a weekend or a week or a month — whatever is appropriate — in being upon the grounds and healing. It will be as a sanctuary amidst — and yet apart from — the world.

# Community

Each community will be a place of great music, both physical music and inner music. There will be vibrational music, healing music, which will be as a remembrance for others of the tones and frequencies which they are.

Those of you who are remembering the healing properties of colors will find yourselves again offering healing unto your brothers and sisters through the medium of colors. Ones will remember their wholeness — healing — by actually being within the frequency of light of different colors.

A multitude of healing approaches will be available through various physical modalities, nutritional belief systems, and the wholing of mind and spirit through emotional integration. There will be many methods of healing. But the greatest of all is the joy which will be felt upon that land because of the freedom of expression. It will no longer be necessary to acquiesce to the constrictions of the world, dying because of adherence to the letter of the law, but rather, living in the spirit of Who you are. You will be out among nature, and if one wishes to call unto the treetops, one will call. If one wishes to whisper unto the birds, one will whisper unto the birds. There will be much attunement with nature.

What you have been feeling at a subtle level as visions will manifest in the fullness of time. It will come to be the perfect vision and expression of Who you are. And you will know the joy and fulfillment of work in which your Heart and soul come alive. For, yes, there will be physical work to be done; there will be the sweat of the brow at times. There will be the creativity of networking, as you call it, and working within (and beyond) the paperwork of agencies. The creative, holy Child will come fully into play.

The seeds have been planted and the process is well under way. It is a process of the Heart which knows not the timetable of the world and cannot be diverted from its eventual unfoldment. There need not be many who will start a community, but you will be surprised, for there are others who are also called unto the vision of community — ones, brothers and sisters who you may not have met yet in physical form, but you will be meeting. They are being called, as it were, to the Family picnic, the great Reunion, and they will be coming within your presence in time.

The physical structures which you will be putting upon the land and into that land will be in harmony with Mother Earth. Some of you have expressed a reluctance to use wood in the building of the structures, indicating a sorrow surrounding the "killing" of trees. This issue brings into clarity the whole meaning of community, and you witness how you are your own teachers. There are certain products, as you would see, which are provided for your use if the use is done with honor and respect. A tree does not know death. It does not look at itself and know that at age forty-five, or whatever, it plans to die. It does not know the meaning of death; it knows only energy in form. It is not as identified with and focused upon *specific* form as you are. The tree expresses as its form until there is a change in form. The tree is one with you and you can be in communication with it, and if you have need of what the tree has to offer, one will go unto the tree and ask it, and the tree will provide. Then, as you see the tree to be expressing in other forms — the wood being used to make other forms — honor the Life energy of that tree in every day. Feel your oneness with it; revere it, honor it as the expression of infinite Life in physicality.

It is the same with what you call the synthetic — consider that word — building materials. You are the one who calls forth everything you behold, and everything, down to the smallest unit of physicality, is energy, Life energy, in form. Build your structures in conscious awareness of the oneness of all Life, with respect and with honor, in communion.

Community is all about oneness. As I and my Father are one, you and my Father are one; you and your Father are one. We are one, and we are one with our holy Mother, the Earth, working in union — which is very necessary when one wants to establish a community — not only with the brothers and sisters at the Heart level, but also in communion with the land and what is growing upon the land. It is a great opportunity, a process of outpicturing oneness.

Know you that it is not necessary that there be a geographical location to which you retreat in order to be a community. For as you commune with your brothers and sisters in the Family which you are, you are aware of the community which you are. Community happens each time you allow yourself to be in communion with yourSelf, individualized as your brothers and sisters. Community happens each time the desire of the heart is to be of service and you place Oneness above singularity. Community happens each time you reconnect with the Family of our Father and enjoy the reunion.

In the days to come you will behold, and be a part of, many communities of the Heart, each one perhaps with a seemingly different focus of service, yet all in communion as the Heart of the holy Child expressing and experiencing the Awakening. If you have had a vision of community, know that you do not have to wait until the physical structures of dwellings, of healing centers, of educational facilities are erected, or that you must take yourself apart into a remote area, before you can experience the community of your Family. Look about you. Whoever stands before you is your Family, and as you allow the constrictions of habitual boundaries to be dissolved, you will experience communion with your brother. This is the true community.

# Earth Changes
## and Predictions

I desire now to speak with you about what you have called the Earth changes. Many of you have asked, "What are these changes which are going to be happening?" Know you well that you are in the midst of these changes. It is not something of the days to come. It is the days which you are living right now, for the changes are happening.

Know you well that you and Mother Earth are not separate. As Mother Earth is coming into Her awakening, as there is an increasing vibration of energy upon the Earth, you also have felt an acceleration within your own being, within your own consciousness. Many of you have talked about how there seems to be less time to do things. There seem to be more and more activities which you want to do and less and less time to do them.

You have registered the acceleration even within the body. And what is changing is an increase in the vibration within the very cells themselves, in the Light which you are allowing to radiate through and within the body. The very DNA of the cells is changing to allow more Light and more frequency to be accommodated.

This is also, in parallel form, happening with Mother Earth as She is increasing in the rate of vibration which She is expressing. Mother Earth, at this time, is immersed in what you would know as a great energy field of Light which is streaming to Her and within Her, and She is responding to the energy as you are registering the acceleration in the cells of your body.

As this occurs with Mother Earth, you, because the molecules of your body, having been attracted from the dust of the Earth, literally, by the consciousness which you are, will feel what is happening with Mother Earth on an intimate level. You have formed the body, the vehicle which you use, from the molecules of physicality. So, as Mother Earth feels changes, you also will be feeling changes. And conversely, and more to the Truth: as your consciousness is accelerating in its own vibration, in its own knowing, this will be registered in the vibrations of Mother Earth. You are not separate from Mother Earth.

For a long time mankind/womankind has forgotten his/her connection with the Earth and has felt that one merely walked upon the surface, and whatever the Earth did was separate from what you were experiencing, and vice versa. However, the belief in separation was not always held to be true. In the beginning when Earth was birthed, you were there. Your consciousness, out of the Oneness which you are with All, helped form and birth the Earth. And at that point you were very much aware of your connection with Mother Earth and with the Light that is one.

You knew this very intimately. But as time, as you have perceived time to be in the illusion of the Dream, has progressed, you have forgotten your connection with Mother Earth. Not all cultures have, but what you have been experiencing in recent linear history has been a forgetting of the true nature of the relationship and a using of Mother Earth with no thought as to what would be best done in partnership in the marriage you have formed.

Not all cultures have forgotten. Even now your native American cultures honor the relationship of man/woman to Mother Earth, and there is a sensitivity to vibrations and an awareness of shared expression of Life.

Mother Earth loves you with a love which is equal to the Love of your Heavenly Father. They are one and the same. Many times I have said unto you that there is no separation. The Love which you are, the Love of the Heavenly Father which birthed you as a great ray of Light, is the same as the Love of Mother Earth, and you are one with Her.

As your consciousness now is awakening, so is the consciousness of the totality of Mother Earth, the Light being upon which you walk. Yes, there will be changes. Yes, there will be shudderings which you will feel. But these need not be experienced in fear. That is not why you are being told this message. You are calling forth the message so that you will understand your oneness with the Earth, so that you can acknowledge your oneness and let others who may not be so attuned know also that there is nothing to fear. Fear arises from the soil of separation.

These messages are not given for the purpose of fear, but mankind/womankind, in its habit, its familiar bias, sometimes forgets Who and What you are and hears it in fear. Know always that you are one with Mother Earth. Know always there is nothing outside of you. Know always that you are in the right place at the right time.

Many of you have asked my mother, Mary, about the Earth changes, and she has talked about the Earth changes in years past. Know that those predictions, those messages which were given at that time were given as it was called forth at that time. There have been changes in the consciousness of mankind which have happened since those messages were given.

The shifts in perception happen moment by moment. What may have been and was true when you left home this morning is no longer the truth because it is ever expanding and ever changing as your consciousness changes. So therefore, messages which were given even as recently as a few months ago are now different because you are allowing changes in your perception of Who you are and what the world is for.

Know that the purpose of the messages was not to cause fear. It was to offer a choice to the holy Son of God, the holy Daughter of God, to look at the messages and to ask, "What is my truth about my relationship with Mother Earth? What is my Truth in all that is happening?"

Know you well that these messages have been given to you so that you may understand the whole vision of what is happening, so that you may prepare to take care of the body — if that be deemed necessary — and that you may prepare to take care of others who may not be so attuned.

This is a great opportunity for being Who you are, for being the Love of the Father and for sharing that Love with others. If there should occur what would be seen as a disaster — and know you well that an occurrence is, to you, as you perceive it — if there should be a need for you to share with others, it is your opportunity to share your love, to comfort them, to be there for them with the physical needs which they may have at that time. That is why you have been told to prepare. Not to prepare for yourself to save your own body. What value is there in that? Many times you have laid down the body and many times you have raised up a new one. Not to prepare to save your own body, but to prepare to do what is needful for others.

It is the same as many have asked about ascension and have seen it as a goal: to ascend, to spiritualize the body so that it can ascend. Ascension is a by-product of knowing Who you are, a by-product of the awakening which is happening. The goal is not the ascension. The goal is the awakening. And if your Heavenly Father calls upon you to make a demonstration as I was called upon to do and to ascend, then you will ascend because the very cells themselves will be so light that they will not be held upon the Earth.

But the goal is not one of ascension, and here with the Earth changes the goal is not to save the body. The body will be saved if that is needful. But the purpose is to share with others the Light which you are and the Love which you are, and through that extension to know that you are more than the body.

It has been seen, in the present point of focus, as desirable to have a body to express with and to be able to use for communication — to communicate the Love and the Light. But the body and the saving of the body is not the goal. That may happen, or it may happen that you will choose to lay down the body. It does not matter. As easy as it is to lay down the body, it is just as easy to raise up a new one, if that is so chosen.

So know that, yes, there are going to be Earth changes as Mother Earth is registering a vibrational shift. There will be shudderings, there will be movement which will happen, but know also that you will always be in the right place at the right time. If you want to know the will of your Heavenly Father for you, just open your eyes and look around. Whoever is in front of you at that moment is the one your Heavenly Father would have you speak to. They are the one your Heavenly Father would have you help in any way you can.

You are the Light and the Love of the Heavenly Father. This is truly Who you are. It matters not whether you express with the physical body, the bag of dust, or if you express with what is called a Light body. Those of you who are attuned can feel the vibrations of the Light beings which are here with you in Love.

Know that you are held in Love, in the arms of the Heavenly Father. You need not fear the changes. At the soul level you have cried out to know, "Who am I? I want to know my whole Self." And your prayers are being answered. When the holy Child desires to awaken, all of creation rearranges itself to facilitate the fulfillment of the desire. Everything upon your path is there because you have asked for it to be there. Everything upon your path, if you will receive it, is a blessing for you. It holds for you the steps to awakening.

The purpose, beloved one, of the acceleration, of the changes, is the Atonement — the At-one-ment of coming Home, in conscious awareness, to your Heavenly Father.

Enjoy the momentary adventure and share with others that the changes are not to be viewed in fear, but from the perspective of the Awakening. Truly, you and many of your brothers and sisters are ones who have lived in the time of what was known as Atlantis and have expressed upon this plane in many, many civilizations. And even though you might choose the laying down of the body, it does not mean the cessation of life, as you have experienced — and they have also — but have forgotten.

The changes to come are not ones of doom and gloom. The changes to come are ones of windows of opportunity, of freedom offered, of awareness of the unlimitedness which you are. For you will stand upon the mountain peak and you will behold all that you have created and you will call it good. The Earth changes are the perfect outpicturing of changes within the consciousness of mankind: the releasing of limiting beliefs, the opening up to new ways of thinking, the shifting of perceptions, the change from time-centered values to timelessness.

The way of the Heart is one which trusts. The way of the Heart is one that knows perfect safety, because the Heart knows that it is always in the right place at the right time. It cannot be otherwise, because you are the one who is calling forth the very experiences which are your pathway Home.

Any time you would perceive an occurrence or a possible occurrence with fear, stop, and ask yourself, "Is this the way of the Heart? Is there another way of looking at this?" And then you will know that, yes, there is another way. You may abide within the very center of your being.

I tell you this now because there have been many questions about the Earth changes and there have been many questions of, "Where should I be? Where should I go? What should I do? Where is it safe?" And I share with you that you are always held lovingly within the arms of your Heavenly Father, and the only thing you need remember is the simplicity of being the Love which you are.

When I behold you, there is such great love that I know for you, for I know Who you are. You are immersed in a sea of Love, in an ever ongoing stream which is Love. You are beautiful. Your radiance extends to the farthest universes and beyond. The universes themselves would not exist without you.

Your safety lies within Who you are. There is nothing that can threaten the holy Child of the Heavenly Father. There is nothing that will take from you, as you would see it, the body. It is always a choice. If the body be laid down, it is a choice to lay it down, and you may later raise up another, as easy as you would now change the raiment.

If you find yourself in the middle of an upheaval, know that your Heavenly Father has asked you to be there as the presence of Love and peace. And as long as you are expressing through the body, be the peace and the Love of the Father and be it in courageousness, for there is nothing which can harm you.

You are eternal. You have brought together the molecules of physicality more times than we can count, you and I. If we were to stay here until the end of what you would see as this lifetime and we would count, one each second, we would still not have counted the many times you have manifested the molecules of physicality with which to express. You have raised up a body and you have laid down the body more times than you can count, and it matters not whether you express with the body or as the Light which you are. For truly, you have expressed as the Light which you are many times as well. You have been others', as you would see it, guardian angel. You have been very busy.

Many of your brothers and sisters worry about the predictions. All predictions can be proved to be true as events unfold. It is much as your world would see in using the statistics; the very numbers themselves can be used to "prove" any equation by using them in a certain manner. And it is the same with the predictions, for you can look back upon the predictions later and say, "Oh, this is what was meant and this is how it fits in to the tapestry which has been woven."

The predictions themselves are ones to be seen in the context of the Dream of the holy Child, who thinks himself/herself to be upon a journey and to be far from the Kingdom. The predictions do not have to be taken as truth themselves, for they are someone's vision of what could be a possible future.

So, what does that do to all the dire prophecies which you have heard? It puts them as a choice, for you will experience yourself coming through what would be the dire prophecies if you feel a need to purify yourself in order to be worthy enough to come unto a place called Heaven upon Earth. And many of your brothers and sisters will choose that path. They will see it as being necessary that they come through harrowing experiences in order to say, "I have been saved," and yet they are the ones saving themselves: "I have been saved for a grander purpose; therefore, I must be more worthy than what I knew myself to be." Well, that is a grand Truth. They are and you are. And there are many who will choose a path of what you would see as hardship and of trauma. But it is not necessary.

The good news which I share with you is that you are already the holy Child of the Heavenly Father, created before time was, and if you desire to manifest Heaven upon Earth this very moment, so be it, and it will be done as you decree it.

You need not go through the upheavals of the volcanoes expressing, and our Holy Mother, the Earth, shaking a bit. You *can* experience that if you like the amusement parks, the roller coasters, the excitement.

You can allow yourself to experience the very shaking of the Earth. You can stand there as a piece of Jell-O would be and go with it, and know yourself to be the holy Child Who is calling it forth and know that you are always safe wherever you be.

Some of your brothers and sisters see the predictions of others to be a probable future because their belief system allows such a probability. And for others the predictions are seen to be very truth itself because they are in alignment with what is being predicted. This is why you can have two standing upon the same street corner who will witness an event and each one will see it from a different perspective. The event itself will be the same but the perception of each one will be different — totally different in some cases.

It depends upon the belief system of the person and whether one is coming from Love, from the Truth of your being, or from fear, the voice of the ego which speaks of separation, which speaks of the possibility of doom and gloom and of the threatening of the physical expression upon this plane.

So one can look upon a prediction and see in it the forecast of fear, of threatening the very life form, or one can look upon the prediction as it is, and see that it is a possible future, one which you have a choice about. For truly, each moment you have a choice as to where you will abide.

There have been many who have gone through what you would see as the volcanic eruption and have continued to express in physicality. What matters most of all is Who you know yourself to be. And as you see the body itself to be an extension of your consciousness, of your belief of Who you are, you need not fear any prediction.

It is not that you and your brothers and sisters have to hurry hither and yon to find a safe place, for truly, you could go unto what is judged a safe place and walk across the street and collide with one of your chariots. Or you could be living in what would be judged an unsafe place and at the last moment find yourself called to travel unto another place and you will not be where the great upheaval occurs. Or you may stay and be the extension of the Love which you are. You are always in the right place at the right time. You are always guided to be where you need to be as the servant of the Heavenly Father. And as you are willing to be the servant, you serve your own Awakening.

So, if you want to have fun with it, that is all it is for. Have fun with it. But if you would see it as being fearful and if you would see it as being threatening, times where the body calls out and says, "This is going to be threatening to me. Preserve me. Save me," then, beloved one, return quickly unto the place of the Heart, the place of peace, the place where you take a deep breath and you connect with Who you are and you decree what you experience. For always you decree what you experience. Therefore, pause and decree in conscious awareness, as the master which you are.

Heaven is here, right where you are. Heaven is now; there is no other time. Be you, therefore, the peace of your Father and extend that Peace to all others. You are the Light of the world.

# Marriage and Relationships

Beloved Child, regarding the custom of marriage, it is truly a happy occasion when two seemingly separate individuals come together in a space where they would declare unto their brothers and sisters that they have found and wish to express love in this form.

It was at a marriage feast where I performed my first recorded miracle, when my mother asked me to demonstrate publicly the power of manifestation through the knowledge of creative oneness. She had come unto me and said that the supply of wine for the wedding feast was becoming depleted. As you know, in the day and time which you shared with me, the wedding feast would go on for days. It was quite a celebration. And the wine had been enjoyed — all of the good wine — and so my mother came unto me and asked would I provide more wine? And, at first, I felt perhaps as you would feel if your mother came unto you and asked you to provide more wine. You would probably say, "Wait until I hop in the car and go down to the nearest store, and I will bring some back."

But in the day and time which we shared it was not that easy to do. The store was not so readily available. It was with surprise that I heard my mother's request, for I had not thought it yet time to publicly declare the beginning of what would become known as my ministry. I knew that manifestation of any substance is not only a possibility but an ongoing truth of reality. I knew from experiences in my travel and study that I could manifest more wine — and my mother knew this, as I had previously done so in the intimacy of our home — but to do so publicly would be an irreversible choice which would forever alter the course of my experience in that lifetime. However, what do you do when faced with a choiceless choice? So I asked the ones who were serving to fill up the wineskins with water. I spoke unto my Father with great faith, which means to stand in the place of Oneness, and saw that the water would manifest itself as wine. When it poured forth as wine, many were astonished at my "magic" — but, you are the Magic in every moment.

We have spoken often of how you are the Child of the Heavenly Father, and the one you see next to you is also the Child of the Father, and the one behind you and the one in front of you. Wherever you are, you are joined in the Love which you are.

It is truly a place of holy relationship when you recognize the Christ in the one in front of you, in the one who is beside you. And when two come together, recognizing the Christ in each other, there is an expanded awareness, a feeling of expansion, a feeling that has been called love. Oftentimes when you go to a wedding, you will see the joy and the love on the faces gathered there. The love which you feel for another — where does it come from? It springs from the Heart. It springs from you.

When you allow the feeling of expansion, of love, to be expressed in its fullness, you are experiencing your true Self. And it matters not whether it be according to what society would dictate unto you — because, as you have discerned, what society says is acceptable in one day and time has changed with various cultures and various time frames. When you feel love for another person, it is your true essence being expressed, being allowed to come forth. And it matters not whether it is expressed from a man to a woman and a woman to a man or between two women or between two men, or between, as you would see, a mother and child or a child and the puppy. The feeling of love is the essence of your Self, so that wherever the circumstance arises where it calls forth from you your true nature, bless it with your true nature; love and love freely.

Love not with the strings attached, but love with a free love which lets the other one be Who they are — lets them go along their path as they need to go, to experience what they need to experience, as a mother does with a child, knowing that the child will go from her, will grow up to have its own experiences, and yet the bond of love remains always.

Relationships, as they are called, mean relating your true nature to the one who you see in front of you, calling forth in your consciousness the true nature of that other one. And as you are experiencing their true nature, you offer to the other one the opportunity for them to experience Who they are as well. For what they can see in you they must necessarily be themselves. It is a great blessing you give unto others when you love them, because you allow them to see that love and by seeing that love and recognizing it, they have opportunity to know that they are Love, and worthy of love, as well.

It does not mean that they will see it immediately, but each time you offer unto them the opportunity to see that Love, it is a great blessing. And it blesses the giver as well as the receiver. Is this not true?

In every relationship, with any one, you will see pictured for you your belief about yourself. You will see pictured for you your belief about the world around you and how you imagine others to see you. If you see others coming unto you in a loving way and expressing love to you, know that you are expressing that love as well. If ones are coming unto you and pushing the buttons as it would be, and this does happen, give thanks first of all for the button which is being pushed and examine what is coming up for you. What is its deeper meaning? What is it saying unto you about your belief about yourself? What is it mirroring for you? — a good term that your world has. What is it mirroring for you?

Look at it with love, for you are Love. Everything that comes up to see is not a fault, but a wound which has come to be healed. And it cannot be healed, made whole, transformed, unless you first look upon it and are aware of it, and then transform it with love for yourself. Everything that comes up, do not judge, but look upon it as you would be the researcher or the student, and ask yourself, "What is this telling me? What old image have I been carrying?" — sometimes for lifetimes — and see it as a wound which is asking for its healing. And you know very well what heals best is love: love of yourSelf.

Know that each person you meet will reflect perfectly to you your belief. In this consciousness you may then thank them for what they are mirroring to you — although at times the gift may not seem such a gift. At times like that, step back from it and look upon it in objectivity as much as you can — and breathe. The breathing will allow you to step back one degree and to look upon the circumstance and the situation with new eyes and to choose anew. For everything which comes up is either love or a cry for love. It is the same within yourself and it is the same within your brother.

Whenever things come up which seem to be "negative," occurrences which seem not to be in a peaceful state, breathe and ask, "How can I see this in a new way? What is being called for?" It is always love, beloved one. It is always a giving of yourself which is being called for in every relationship. It is a giving of your Self, which is truly a blessing unto you for then you know the wellspring of the Self which you are. For you have to dig deep and allow it to flow. And as it flows, it blesses you.

Look upon everything which transpires within your life as an act within the play. You are all great actors upon the stage. You have picked up a script when you came into, as you would see, this lifetime, and you have agreed that you would be upon this stage and you would act what the part was.

Now, it has not all been written out for you. You are great at improvisation. You do it all the time. You have a choice in every moment to write your own lines within this script, and you do this moment by moment, for you are always free. You are free to look beyond the limitations of what the world would dictate to you. You are free to look beyond the limitations of what your parents and society have taught you. You are free to go beyond the books and the workshops which you have attended and the other friends who have shared freely with you of their insights. You are free in every moment to go within the Heart and to know the wisdom, the unlimitedness which you are.

We have spoken often that you are much more than the body that sits upon the chair and much more than the personality with which you identify in this time and place. There is only a small percentage of you that is focusing upon this part in the play. You are very busy, as you would see it, at the same time in other universes, upon other stages, expressing the grand villain, expressing the great warrior, expressing the great lover, expressing the Love which you are — all of the infinite varieties of expression of the Mind of God. You are the Mind of God expressing upon this plane. You are the Love of the Heavenly Father shining your Light in this world for others to see and for yourself to know.

And as you share your love with others, the miracle which occurs is that you know it to be yourself, for you cannot share with others what you are not already. It is within you. It is you. You are not separate. And as you allow your true Self to come forth and to feel its fullness, then you, in your consciousness, are aware of the Love which you are and you bring this unto every relationship.

Now, there may be times in a relationship that the emotions you are feeling within your own heart are so veiled that it takes a bit of time, as you would see it, to get through — and yet the time, I say unto you, is but a twinkling of an eye.

All of you have said that you want to get through these veils very quickly: "This is the lifetime that I will come unto knowing that I am the Child of the Heavenly Father. I will claim my divine inheritance. I will know it in its fullness." And you have set yourself upon the path, which is, as you have felt already, very much accelerating. And the veils which were seen to be very thick in what you would know as other lifetimes are now very, very thin. So when you see something coming up for you in front of you, it is not a boulder anymore. It is not the mountain, but it is the thinnest of gossamer and you may push it aside easily.

Relationships are a great blessing unto you and to the one who is in front of you. Each time a person comes and shares a path with you, it is an opportunity for you to see the healing which you are. It is an opportunity for you to extend what you would see as healing unto another. And as you extend the healing, it is not only one heart which is healed, but two — and then it expands like the ripples upon a pond and touches others. This is why the Awakening is accelerating: because of the rippling, touching others. Nothing is ever done in isolation.

Never hide yourself from anyone. Never turn away from an opportunity to express love in any way: the smile, the eyes which say, "Yes, I understand," the arm which goes around someone's shoulder and says, "I have been there, too. I care." Sometimes just standing in quietness with another one until they are able to come to a place of peace. Sometimes just reaching out the hand and taking another one's hand just to let them know that you are there for them — the simplest of gestures. And even if this one be not in a place of accepting that love, stand and be the Love which you are. Do not turn away, for what one is calling for at that time is love — even though they may not allow themselves to accept it.

So, do not turn away, but just stand and love in quietness. And as you extend unto that one the opportunity to be in peace, you give them a great opportunity to come to the place of healing: not only healing of the body — which will happen — but healing of the emotions and of the spirit. The healing of the body will follow the healing of the emotions and of the spirit, the soul.

Stand in quietness and in love and breathe, and extend to others the peace which you are. Even if they are in some violence of throwing out the emotions and seemingly pouring it forth to the universes, if you stand in confidence and in your peace, they will come unto a place where they will return to peace themselves. It is the wonderful gift which you give unto others — and in the giving unto others, you are also the receiver.

In what would be termed marriage, it would seem that two have come together in a special relationship where they would see each other as being special and set apart from the others. This is the first step in recognizing the true Love which you are. And at first you find it so kindled because you feel it to be outside of yourself, and you feel the love welling up inside and it has to be shared with another. Know you that that Love is you. That is the Love which you are. And as you share that love with another, falling in love, being in love, the feeling of such exuberance you cannot wait to see another, to share time, to share activities, to share even the smallest details of what you would see as the daily living, to share yourself with another, this is the first step in recognizing the divine Love which you are, and it is a great blessing. And a greater blessing comes forth when you are able to see that the two of you are journeying upon the path together and that you are equals. You are the Light and the Love of the Heavenly Father, and so are your brothers and your sisters. And you will see yourself joined with that one as a team which is extending Love unto others, and you will see the Christ not only in the special one, but in all others who come to share your path — either, as they say, crossing your path or journeying with you.

Then you recognize that it has never been necessary to have a special relationship, for all relationships are special in their holiness as you look upon them in the Light of the Christ. The expanded awareness of knowing Who you are, and seeing the Christ of your brother and sister, illumines each relationship with holiness which banishes exclusive specialness.

Many in your world would look unto relationships and to marriage for the fulfillment of needs, of aspects which they would feel were perhaps lacking or missing, and they would look unto another to fill that seeming need. Know you that no other can fill a seeming need because there is not the need. You are whole and perfect as your Father created you to be. The only thing which you would need, perhaps, is to recognize your wholeness within yourself, but it is not that another one seemingly outside of you can fulfill this for you. It is your recognition of the wholeness, of the holiness, which you are that fulfills any seeming need.

This is why so many of your brothers and sisters try one relationship and it works for awhile, according to what they feel the criteria would be, and then it is discarded and then they are on to another relationship, hoping to get from someone else what is seemingly not there — and yet, all is there — and they will go from relationship to relationship, always seeking, always asking another to, "Fulfill me. Make me complete." And yet, your completeness was established before time began, as your Father's perfect creation.

Further, it is not that you need a special person to share this with. For when one comes unto the realization of the Child of the Father which you are and knows the total wholeness, unlimitedness, of the joy you are, you will go forth and share this freely with all. It will not matter whether they are, as you would see, attached or unattached, whether they are tall or short or fat or thin or seemingly wise or sensitive or whatever. You will go upon your path so full of Love that you cannot contain it, and you will give unto others freely because you know that as you pour it out, more is given to you.

That is what is called holy relationship, because you know that you are whole and you know that your brother and sister is whole, and you share of yourself because you cannot contain it. You cannot hold it back. So, it does not matter whether they be of certain dimensions or certain specifications. You go freely and you share the smile with everyone, as the child smiles and plays upon the playground. For you are the Child of the Heavenly Father and you are playing upon the playground of expression within this reality. Go freely and share of Who you are.

Many have asked me about soulmates and, "Is there a special one, a special soulmate, either in body for me at this time or somewhere in the unseen realms who will come into a body and be with me and will complete me?" You do not need what you would see as a soulmate to complete you. You are already all that is.

Yes, you have a soulmate. It is the one sitting next to you. It is the one behind you. It is the one in front of you. It is the one you talk to in your times of meditation, of prayer, the times when you speak unto one who would be as a friend — perhaps you can see them, perhaps you do not — but one you would speak to as a friend. That is your soulmate. That is you.

Now, you may name this one a special name and you may look for this one in bodily form, and I say unto you: when you come to the place of realizing the Child of the Heavenly Father which you are and you are so full of the Love which you are that you cannot contain it, you will find your soulmate in front of you immediately. And as you begin to share your love with them, you will find it easy to share with another one and another one and another one. There will be no lack of love in your life because you will be outpouring the Love which you are, and you will know multitudinous soulmates.

So yes, there is a soulmate for you, but the secret — which is not hidden from you — is that the soulmate is you, for all minds and all hearts are joined and you are not separate. Although you would see the bodies to be separate, the hearts are not separate, and the Love which you are is so full that it is felt by the trees as you pass by, by the birds you talk to, by your brothers and sisters you see in the grocery store and at the gas station, everyone you meet. You are your own soulmate. And if it pleases you to talk unto a soulmate, know that this is all well and good, but know that the soulmate is not separate from you. The soulmate is you.

That is why you can speak with great ease unto a soulmate: because the soulmate is ever with you. It could not be otherwise. The soulmate rides with you within the chariot, upon the horse, upon the wind in joy, and the soulmate shares everything with you, knows everything with you, because the soulmate is you — closer to you than the body. So, as you feel the joy of the soulmate, know that you are that joy. Where else is that joy welling up? It is not somewhere in the ethers, but it is within your own Heart. It is you.

So when ones would ask of me, "Is a soulmate real?" Yes, that soulmate is as real as you are — and I assure you that you are real. And I do not speak here of the body and the personality. I speak here of the Love and the divine energy which you are. You are very much Real.

Each time you come together and you share the hugs, you are expressing the Light of Reality, intermingling with each other, in conscious awareness, the energy which you are. You can feel it in physical form. And as you feel that energy, then you know you are not limited to what you identify as the skin and the body. Bodies are the vehicle of the ego to say unto you that, "This is all there is. This is the boundary of one individual, separate from another." And yet, this is not true. The energy which activates the body is boundless.

Bodies can be seen to have boundaries, can be seen to be individualized, to be in boxes, as it would be. Bodies can never join. Bodies can share with each other touching, but bodies can never join. Even in the most physical act of joining, it is not a true joining. The divine energy which you are, the Love which you are, cannot help but be joined.

Whenever you are in a relationship — any time that you see someone in front of you, you are in a relationship, however momentary it may be — what you are feeling is your own consciousness. It is what you are bringing forth to that relationship. And it is with great freedom that you may be whatever you want to be. Share your Light freely with others and be the blessing to them. And as you do that, know that you have turned on many others' Lights because you have been outrageous enough to love, to smile, to break forth in laughter, to uplift another.

Think not, in times of what you call despair, depression, that your life has small meaning. You have touched many in what you would see as just this lifetime — and I assure you this is not the only lifetime you are acting in at this moment. You are very active.

All relationships offer you the opportunity to be consciously the Christ that you are. All relationships. Each moment, as it comes up in front of you, offers you a choice of, "Where will I be? Will I be in love or will I be in fear? Will I be in love or will I be coming from a place where I need to prove my separateness?" Each time that you choose for love, you allow the veil to become even thinner, and you walk through it as the molecules go through in osmosis, back and forth. It is that simple and that easy, as you are willing to trust yourSelf.

Relationships are a vehicle which you have manifested for yourself upon this plane to mirror for you your belief about yourself and about others. To see the Love, or fear, reflected in another who would seemingly be separate from you, and yet, they are not. How can you understand what another one is going through if you are not connected? You very much understand what another one is feeling. And yes, it may be because you have experienced it either, as you would see it, in this lifetime or another lifetime. But in Truth it is because the energy which you are is not separate from the energy of what would be seen to be another one. As you are allowing the veils to become as gossamer, you are able to tune into others even without the words and to know what they are feeling, and to allow the shutters of the Heart to be flung wide open.

In every relationship be the Love which you are. All of you are flowers in the garden of our Heavenly Father. All of you are as the stars in the heavens. You shine with a radiance which is beautiful to behold. With the physical eyes it is as you may have put on the dark sunglasses: there is not that much of the Light to be seen. And yet, it can be seen: the aura, as it is called, around a body can be seen with the physical eyes. And know you that you are much brighter than any aura which the physical eyes can see. Look with the eyes of Spirit and behold the holy Light you are.

In every relationship look for the Light that is in it. For there you will find yourSelf. There you will find the joy that is just waiting to be shared freely with others. You are truly holy. You lack for nothing. You need no one else to be in your life to make you whole.

Your world has taught you that to be happy there must be a companion, that there must be someone to share with. And this longing comes from the desire to share from the Heart the Love of the Father. There is nothing wrong in that desire. But it does not mean that it has to be reserved for only one special person. It means that it must be shared with whoever is in front of you at that moment. Do not limit your love.

Pour freely the Love which you are upon whoever is in front of you. You are the Love of the Heavenly Father. Share it freely, because as you share it, you are in-filled with the flow of that Love. You cannot be without it, because you are the Love. But for mankind to experience Love and to know Love, it must be expressed. This is why I have said unto you many times to extend love: because in the extension, then you know the Love you are. It is not for you to sit upon a meditative cushion somewhere in a cave and to be the Love, which you have done in other lifetimes. It is for you now to be out in what you would see as your world, sharing Love freely with others, healing others by the Love which you are.

Your world cries out to you for healing, for love. Your mission, should you choose to accept it, is to consciously be the Love which you are and to share it so freely that others will know the Love they are. Do not be afraid to reach out and touch others, to say, "I love you. I love you because I know Who you are. And I know Who you are because I know Who I am." Be bold; you can say this to others. Your world is crying out for it.

Every relationship is a love relationship when you allow yourSelf to be given freely.

# The Divine Feminine
# in Expression

**A**s there is a new awareness dawning upon your plane, a desire for balance, equality in all aspects, a desire to know and experience Totality of Self, it is appropriate that we speak of the Divine Feminine in expression. And does this mean just the women you would see? No, it does not. For verily I say unto you: the Divine Feminine is an aspect of all of you. Whether you have chosen to express in this lifetime with the form of the male, there is still the Divine Feminine of you.

For truly, all of you have chosen the design pattern of the male and of the female in countless lifetimes. You have expe-

rienced all. You have experienced being the grand warrior —
both with the form of the male and also with the form of the
female, as, for example, what you have called the Amazon
women. Even unto this day and time, you have experienced
being the father; you have experienced being the mother; you
have experienced all.

You are the Divine Feminine in expression. And what
would that be? That is, beloved one, the expression of the
Heart upon this plane, the expression of the Love which you
are. The Divine Feminine is seen in the expression of the
allowance which you give unto yourself and to others, as one
will abide in the Heart and allow another one their path, their
journey, their choices, even if it be choices which you would
judge not so comforting, and yet it is what they have chosen to
experience in order to come again to the place of their Heart.

The Divine Feminine is seen in the appreciation of beauty
in whatever form it appears: in what you would see as the
structures which are built, as in architecture; it is seen in the
landscaped gardens, the fountains of flowing water; it is seen
in the beauty of a sunset or a sunrise; it is appreciating the
process of a flower, the life of a tree; it is appreciating the
innocence and laughter of the small child; it is honoring and
accepting the love of a beloved pet; it is acknowledging the
smile upon another's face and the love Light in the eyes; it is
beholding in reverence all of Life expression upon this plane
— and all other planes that you can imagine, knowing that
there are worlds within worlds and universes within universes
— and it is allowing your own consciousness to expand,
abiding in the Heart as the peace which you are.

The Divine Feminine is peace, the peace which passes the
understanding of the world. It is not the understanding of the
mind which brings you unto the peace of the heart, for the

mind will love to play with concepts, ideas, rationale, arguments, until finally there is a time where it pauses for a moment and allows you to dip into the peace of the Heart.

The Divine Feminine means abiding in peace. And as you abide as Peace, you find with ease there can be the allowance of all things and there can be the appreciation of all things, for you can look beyond the appearances of the world; you can look beyond to the broader vision which sees with the eyes of Christ, sees with the eyes of eternity, beholding that there is an order — even in seeming chaos and confusion — although, sometimes when you would stand so close to it, with the nose pressed against the event, it is hard to see the order in it.

The expression of the Divine Feminine allows you to step back from the event and to behold the eternal vision, to be able to see everything as the grand tapestry which brings the sleeping Child to wakefulness. You are the child, experiencing new adventures, allowing yourself to get in touch with the Child, the holy Child which you are, the whole Child.

The expression of the Divine Feminine allows you to come unto the place which has been known as intuition or intuitive knowledge. It is the inner wisdom. It is allowing the inner wisdom to come forth from a place which is not of the world. It is not of the teaching you would have in front of you in a book or what has been taught to you by others. But it comes from within. It has been called "intuition" — the inner tuition, or inner teaching.

You have experienced times when you knew something was going to happen, and, sure enough, it came to pass, or you thought about someone and shortly thereafter they contacted you. In those moments you have expanded into your inner knowing. You have relaxed the constraints of what the analytical mind would accept as "true" or rational.

Those of you who would be — and are — healers dip deeply into the Divine Feminine to bring forth the intuitive qualities which allow you to facilitate another's healing. It is not that you do the healing, but you are there as a friend to allow the healing energy to come forth, and if it be received, there is the wholing which takes place. The other one, as it would be seen, receives the wholeness which they are — an awareness of the wholeness they are — and there being no longer a perceived need for the disease, it is released.

At times like that, you are very much dipping into the Divine Feminine, for the Divine Feminine is the healer, the One who knows the wholeness, the One who is as the mother who sees a child learning, experiencing, making choices, and loves that child throughout all experiences, knowing that the child is whole, knowing that the child will grow in wisdom and in stature.

And it does come to pass, that as you grow in wisdom and in stature — there's not always a relationship there, but quite often there is — one comes to the place of recognizing one's own Divine Feminine aspects. Such a recognition is being called forth upon this plane at this time.

You have seen and you have heard from your brothers and sisters a great crying out for healing. Healing of the body, yes, for there are many of what you call diseases upon this plane, but more so there is a calling out to know the wholeness of the Child. For truly, the wholeness of the body will be established when they know Who they are and no longer see a need for the dis-ease.

Many are calling out for healing of the emotions, healing of what can be seen as a very deep sorrow held within the minds of mankind since the beginning of time, from the time when you first forgot to remember, from the time when the holy Child first thought to go upon a far journey and thought himself/herself to be far from the Kingdom of our Heavenly Father. And there has been a sorrow held within the mind, registered even at what you call the soul level: a longing to come Home again.

It is a sorrow which wells up and you know not why it comes forth. And you sit and you abide with it and you ask, "Is it something that happened today? Or is it something that happened last week? Or a year ago? Was it this lifetime?" And you think and you cannot quite put your finger on it, but there is a sorrow. It is the sorrow of the holy Child thinking himself or herself to be far from the Heavenly Father's Love, and yet, the Divine Feminine knows that instantly as you abide in the Heart you are Home.

That is what the Divine Feminine is all about. It is returning Home. It is the Love which you are. The word "love" has been used so often that it conveys only part of the meaning. It symbolizes the whole meaning of the Love which you are, but unlimited meaning is incomprehensible to the mind, for the mind accepts concepts as boxes with labels, ideas, something which can be grasped and can be looked at in various ways and analyzed.

To know the Love which you are requires that you go unto the stillness and peace of the Heart, and there, abiding in the sacredness of one's own Being, communing with the Light, you allow yourself to experience an expansion of feeling, an expansion of Love. The love which you feel for another one is part of it. The love which you feel for a beloved pet is part of it. That knowing of love gives you a clue, a hint.

The Love which you are transports you momentarily — and even longer if you will allow it — out of this world, out of the narrow focus which would see the events of this world as being all there is. It brings forth an exhilaration, a feeling which has been called bliss, and yet those are just words until the experience comes and is known within the Heart.

Not in the heart as a muscle. Not in the heart even as you would see it as a chakra, but in the Heart as a symbol for all of the divine energy which you are. And as you allow yourself to soar in your imagination, you allow yourself to experience Love. It is unconditional. It is unconceptualized. It is a feeling of connectedness, a feeling of energy, expanded energy, and yet to try to explain it, to put it into words, takes it from unlimitedness to limited knowing. But once you have experienced it, you never forget.

And what is occurring upon this plane at this time is a grand remembrance, remembering how to come Home. Coming Home is the Divine Feminine. It is that quiet place. It is that place called Home. More than just the house in which you would live. More than just what you would call the home of your family, and yet it is family — the Family of all.

The holy Child has desired to experience form in the molecules of physicality, in the dust of our Holy Mother, the Earth. You are the creator of matter, of what you see in form. You are the creator of the form, and you have desired to experience what it feels like to activate matter upon this plane. You have desired on other dimensions or planes, as you would see them, to experience what it feels like to be other forms of expression. But upon this plane, upon our Holy Mother, the Earth, you have desired to know what it feels like to be the Spirit, the Energy which you are, activating the molecules of physicality.

What does it feel like to be a dinosaur? For truly you have experienced what that feels like. Can you imagine how it would feel to be that size? All different forms, even of dinosaur or tiny insect, are your creation and your experience.

Upon this plane, because of the form of matter, there has often been an intensity of attention paid to the form, where the Spirit that you are, activating the form, has forgotten that you/Spirit are the one who is driving the car, that you/Spirit are the one who is activating the body.

Oftentimes it was seen as necessity to save the form. The body, as you know, has a grand way of calling out when it would be in danger. And there has been much attention paid to the form and the matter, which has accentuated that which you call the masculine, the activity that would be seen to be necessary for the ongoingness of the matter.

But there is coming — and it is well under way — a wave of awareness upon this plane which is calling forth now the Divine Feminine, to bring into balance both aspects. For truly, as you would experience the Energy that you are, the Light that you are in form, there needs to be and is coming a balance which will bring forth the feminine aspect, to balance the honoring of both form and energy. There is not a denial of the activity which keeps form in expression, the activity that would be known as masculine, for truly, the masculine is divine as well. Now there is a desire for balance, bringing about the true marriage of divine Masculine and Feminine qualities.

Many of your brothers and sisters are now feeling a desire to do what is known as meditation, to sit in quietness and to connect with the Heart, to connect with peace, and then to come from that place in activity, in expression, in a balancing. For you are all expressing the Divine Feminine and the Divine Masculine. It matters not what design pattern you have chosen to express with in this lifetime, for truly you have chosen to be the male/female in other lifetimes, and what you desire now to express is the marriage, the union.

And what will that union birth upon this plane? If you will receive it, it will birth Heaven on Earth. It will birth a time of great Light, even to the physical eyes, the light of wonderful auras, for you will see others as the Light which they are. Yes, you will see physical form, for there will still be the expression with the physical form, but you will behold more of the Light which they are — and which you are — being received and radiated through the very cells themselves. You will see Light around the plants and the trees, around the flowing water, around everything you have created. It will be seen with the physical eyes, as they are undergoing a change, and it will be heard even with the physical ears.

There will be a harmony of the vibrations which will be heard, not as a cacophony of sounds which you often have now upon this plane: as the sounds of the honking of the chariots on your freeways — are they free ways? — and as the sounds which come on what are known as your airwaves. There is much that one could term a cacophony. There will be evolving more harmonious sounds. You will hear the very wind in the trees. You will hear the vibration of a plant as it grows, if you choose to. But it will not be that you will hear so much that there will be a confusion.

You will know yourself to be vibration, and you will know yourself to be the order which brings forth the harmony of the vibrations. And you, as the energy that goes forth, even as you will take a step, you will know the vibration that is set in motion as you walk through the air molecules. You are in vibration right now, and there will come a time — and it comes rapidly —when you will be able to hear your vibration even with the physical ears, if you so choose.

From the growing awareness of shared sound, vibration, will evolve a greater sense of oneness, for as you can behold and hear your own vibration and the vibration of others, you will know yourself to be no longer separate. It will be as the symphony playing together. For it will be necessary that you play together — yes, beloved one — on several levels: playing together as the music which you are, yes, and playing together as the Child which you are.

It will be all that you have imagined Heaven on Earth to be, and you are the very ones who are calling it forth. You are the ones who are manifesting it. It is not ones such as I, Jeshua ben Joseph, or other masters that you would see, other great entities afar off somewhere, who are going to come and gift this upon your plane. For that is not our job. It is not even something that we can do.

You are the ones who are calling it forth and you are the ones who will experience it — and we will experience it with you for we are not separate from you. Even as I speak of a "we", it would connote separation. That is the problem with words.

You are calling forth the balance of the Divine Feminine and the Divine Masculine as the whole Child that you are, the holy Child of our Heavenly Father, the Creator, from Whom you are never separate. For if you are Life — and I assure you that you are — you are your Father's creation, and you are your Father's expression. You are your Father's Child: Son or Daughter.

The Divine Feminine calls forth a love and a reverence for our Holy Mother, the Earth, an awareness of what would be known as ecological issues, where it is seen to be of value to honor and reverence every living form. And know you that the ones which have been known as extinct will come back again as you call them forth. They will come back and be experienced again upon this plane.

The ones known as the unicorns are just waiting for you and your brothers and sisters to call them forth. They are waiting, as it would be, in the wings. Also the flying horses, the Pegasus, will be here again.

For it is not by accident that you think of these forms. These are forms which you have experienced in what you would see as other lifetimes. These are forms that you have, if you will receive it, experienced being in other lifetimes. That is why you can feel a oneness, why they are not foreign to you. You can understand how it would feel to fly as the grand horse. These will be called forth again upon this plane as you desire them.

You will know how to feed yourself instantly. It will be as with the loaves and fishes: you will stretch forth your hand and what you need for nourishment of the physical body will be there. For you will think it, and as you think it, it will be there.

It happens even now, beloved one, except that you believe in a process of time which would say that there needs to be the seed which is planted and it needs to grow, and it needs to be harvested, processed, and then it comes through what you call as several of the middle men, unto your grocery store where you buy it and then it feeds you. You will see a process of bringing that closer together — instantaneously — for time will no longer be seen as necessary upon this plane.

Time is seen now as a belief in process which says there must be a beginning and probably a long middle and then you come to completion. But soon manifestation will be seen and experienced as it is upon other planes and dimensions, where you think a thought and instantly it is manifest in front of you.

You have served yourself with the belief in process so that you can get your priorities straight before everything is instantly manifest. For you know there are times when you will worry about something. You will go through the "what ifs" — "What if this were to happen? Oh, my God, if this happens...." And if you did not have the belief in process that delays manifestation of thought, instantly you would be into whatever you have feared.

So you have given unto yourself the gift, as it would be, of the belief in process so that you can try out the ideas without being instantly into the manifestation. You can play around with it and if you do not like how it feels, you can choose anew.

But there is coming upon this plane a time when there will no longer be the need or the belief in process, and instantly as you think something, it will be manifest. So I would suggest that you be very vigilant as to what you are thinking, what you are worrying about, and ask yourself, "Is this truly where I would like to abide?" And if it is not, know that you can choose anew. You have the power of choice. As the creative holy Child, the Child of the Creator, you have the power to recreate.

# Divine Feminine

You have seen upon this plane a growing reverence for what has been known as the Goddess, a remembrance of honoring, as in what you would see as ancient times, the Divine Feminine. The worship of the Goddess and Her aspects acknowledges the desire for balance and integration of the Totality of yourSelf, expressing and honoring both the attributes which would be seen as masculine, historically symbolized by God, and the qualities of the feminine, seen as Goddess.

Now, as the Divine Feminine, call forth your intuitive qualities, your healing qualities, the quality of Love, the quality of compassion, the quality of appreciation of beauty, the quality of allowance, the quality of peace and mercy and faith, the quality which abides with all things, knowing that there is an order to everything, the quality which believes, as the optimist does, that the glass is half full rather than half empty.

The question has been asked if ever I experienced and expressed as a woman upon this plane. What would you say to that, beloved one?

Yes, definitely. Not I as Jeshua ben Joseph the personality, but I as the Christ energy that I am and that you are, I have expressed many times upon this plane as woman. For I desired to know what it feels like to be the handmaiden, to serve what would be known as the man.

I desired to know how it would feel to have a man come unto me and want me and to say that he would do anything for me. I experienced it. I found that I desired equality.

But I experienced all — as you have — because I wanted to know all: how it felt to give birth to a child, how it felt to lose a child; how it felt to lose a mate — and one does not have to be a woman to experience that. And I wanted to know how it feels to give of your heart to one so that you would lay down the very body for that one if it meant that they would come Home — and I did that in lifetimes.

And then I came unto the expression which you have so well known, as Jeshua ben Joseph, to experience what it feels like to lay down the body and to raise it up again so that all of us, as the Child of our Heavenly Father, know that we are Life, eternal Life, that we are the one who calls forth the beautiful design pattern which you have chosen, that calls it forth in every moment to express, and that it is only a belief which says that the body will be laid down and will stay down. It is a very deeply held belief but it is not the Truth. It is a truth, with a small "t," but it is not the Truth.

The Truth is that you are the creative Energy which has called forth the body in the first place, and when you choose to lay it down, you will lay it down and it will be a choice. And if you choose in the next moment to raise it up, or if you choose after some days, as was with my brother Lazarus, to then raise it up, it will be raised up. For you are the Energy which activates the body — not the other way around, although the body at times will call out and say that it is the master. It is not.

Many of you are experiencing being the master of the body. Many of you who are counting many years and yet keeping the youth of the body, know that you revitalize the body every moment, knowing that as you think yourself — not only thinking with the mind, but thinking with the heart, the belief — as you know yourself to be Life, you do not age.

You express in your prime, as you choose. This is what we as masters do when we come and choose a body to express with momentarily: we see ourselves as being in the prime —

unless it suits a purpose to come in another form, for the one that we are conversing with.

When I manifest a body upon this plane — which I do from time to time for the fun of it, for the interchange of talking with one — I manifest a body which is in perfect health, in its prime, as you would call it, perfection, of wholeness, a body that looks like perhaps it has worked out, been out in communion with the angel of sun. Or if need be, I manifest a body which would sit next to one in a very unassuming way and allow the heart to be wide open so that the other one knows that they are safe to share with me.

You manifest your body in every moment. It is new in every moment as you choose to manifest it. And beautiful it is. It is a delight.

You are the master upon this plane. You are calling forth the Divine Feminine of your Self. You are calling it forth in order to know your wholeness, to no longer deny aspects of your Self, but to gather them all in, as it would be, in conscious awareness. It is not that they have been scattered off somewhere separate from you, but you are bringing them in in conscious awareness, to know your whole Self. And as you do that, beloved one, you call forth Heaven upon Earth.

You have heard me say that I and the Father are one. And this is True. You and the Father are one. But the way that the holy Child has chosen in this age to remember and to come Home to the Father is through the integration of the Divine Feminine, of remembering the Mother which is the Heart.

I have been asked why I chose, in the lifetime of Jeshua ben Joseph, to speak so often of my relationship with the Father. It spoke a language — and still does to some extent — that ones could relate to. It was the way of the society itself at that time to put the attention and the focus upon the male, the masculine, and that is what has been recorded in your Scriptures, as you know them. And it has been reinforced by many of the male priests and the religious organizations who have held it to be of value that woman be seen as either an object to be owned, something useful perhaps, a servant, an ornament, and that was all. What you are calling forth now is the recognition of equality as the holy Child, honoring both the masculine and the feminine.

The Divine Feminine is the peace of the heart that comes forth after the storm of the emotions, after the mind has exhausted its chatter. You know it well. I also, in the lifetime as Jeshua ben Joseph, experienced the mind of chatter, being full of questions, searching the Scriptures, asking questions of the rabbis, of my teachers, until finally they said to me, "Jeshua," — or, as they called me, "Yeshua," — "go sit by flowing water and discern for yourself the answer."

Sometimes I thought they wanted to be rid of me — and perhaps they did. But there was a grand wisdom in their suggestion, for as I sat by flowing water and as I knew myself to be one with the very energy of the water, as I knew myself to be one with the trees and the plants which grew by the side of the water, I allowed the Heart to open and the inner wisdom to come forth. I allowed the mind to become quiet.

That is the Divine Feminine in expression: allowing the mind to become quiet and returning again unto the place of the Heart, where all wisdom abides. Honor the divine Feminine of yourself as you honor the Father. Call forth into balance all aspects of yourSelf. Then, verily, you will know Heaven upon Earth and you will be Home.

# Divine Feminine

# Seek Ye First
# The Kingdom

**B**eloved Friend, remember in each moment your holiness, for you lack for nothing. There is no one who can harm you. There is no one who can take from you or diminish you. In times of turmoil, doubt and confusion, in times of sorrow, turn unto me. For in turning unto me, I will remind you of the holiness that you are and that I am and that we share because we are one. You can never be alone and you can never lack for anything. Truly, you are the beloved Child of our Heavenly Father.

"Seek ye first the Kingdom of Heaven." Oftentimes this was my message unto you when we walked the Earth together.

For if you will go first unto the place of the Heart, you will find the Kingdom within. It is not to be sought upon the mountaintop. It is not to be sought afar off from you. It is not to be sought in great books. It is not to be sought in workshops. It is not to be sought in lifetimes of spiritual retreat unto the monasteries to be a monk, a recluse — although it can be found there and has been. The mountaintops, the books, the workshops, the retreats serve as catalysts for remembrance that after all is said and done — quite literally — the Kingdom is within.

The Kingdom of our Father is to be found within the Heart. When you tire of the activity of the world, when you have exhausted all of the avenues of drama and you return again unto the peace of the Heart, you find the Kingdom where it has always been. And as you find the peace and inspiration within, there is such a feeling of expansion that you need to share it with others, and you go as the joyful child upon your way, sharing it with whoever is in front of you at any moment. You become the Light switch for many others' Lights as they come unto you.

I say this to you: you are coming unto such a place of realization that the joy within you will be full and overflowing. It has been said that this is a New Age and yet, I say unto you: it is the age of Remembrance of what has always been. It is the age of Light, and you are coming to a realization of the Light that cannot even be contained within the very cells of the body and must be shared — the Energy which you are must be shared in a great freedom of expression, because you will not be able to contain it.

Seek ye first the Kingdom of Heaven, and all else will be added unto you. Seek ye first your true nature, and you will know that you *are* All. When the voice of the world will come and knock upon the door of your mind, demanding attention, demanding answers, demanding action, return quickly unto the place of the Heart, there abiding in silence, listening for the still small Voice, the Voice of inner wisdom, which is You. Then the peace that passes the understanding of the world will be yours and you will know yourself to be the Child of the Heavenly Father. In this knowledge all the cares and concerns of the world are seen in true perspective. Not denied, but seen against the backdrop of the tapestry of Eternity, seen to be within the context of the Dream.

How do you return quickly unto the peace of the Heart? With the simplicity of the breath.

Breathe with me now. Breathe in the golden white Light that you are, easily, effortlessly, deeply. Feel the peace descending, enfolding you in a cloud of Love.

{Pause.}

Breathe in the golden white Light that you are. Take it very deeply within the very cells of the body and feel the vitalization that happens as the Light touches every cell of the body.

{Pause.}

Breathe in the golden white Light that you are, and with each exhale, exhale the Love that you are unto your brothers and sisters, unto the whole of the world.

{Pause.}

Never doubt that the Voice of Spirit will be heard. Never doubt that the wake-up call will be heard — for it has been heard. Your coming Home is inevitable, and I stand at the threshold to greet you. I reach out my hand to take yours.

Seek ye first the Kingdom of Heaven. It is the place of peace within. It is the place where you realize, and know with total knowingness, that you are one with the Father, that you are His expression, utilizing the vehicle of the body to express. Return momently to the place of peace within the heart. Remember your holiness.

When you pray unto your Heavenly Father, do not ask Him for material goods. Do not pray unto Him for a car, for a house, for your Heavenly Father does not have material goods to give to you. It is not that He would withhold from you, but He does not have a car, a house, the material possessions to give unto you. When you pray unto your Father, do not ask for health. Do not ask for companionship. Do not ask for wealth. For I say unto you: you already have these. It is Who you are. You lack for nothing. It is not that the Heavenly Father would not answer a prayer. It is always being outpoured for you; it is Who you are as His Child.

In Truth, whatever you would desire at any moment you have and you are. And yet, in the desiring you are saying that you do not have it and that it must be apart from you. Pray knowing that you have received. This is the true prayer.

Pray in gratitude to your Heavenly Father for what you already are and what you already have, because truly, you are the holiness of the Child of our Father. You lack for nothing. So when you would pray unto our Heavenly Father, pray only for the awareness and the realization of what you already are, of your holiness. And yet, do not pray in a manner of supplication, that He would have something that He could give unto you that you have not. Pray in gratitude, in knowing that you already have and that you already are. Do you see the difference?

When you recognize a desire within the heart — and there is nothing wrong in recognizing a desire, for this is truly the message of the soul speaking unto you — recognize what the desire is and then pray in gratefulness that you already have received, because you already have what you are desiring. It takes only a shift in perception, the simple choice to acknowledge that you have it, to behold all in a new Light. You have all power: all power of healing, because you are already whole. You have already all power of manifestation. Anything that you would ask for and truly desire to have manifest within your realm is within your power to manifest — anything.

So if there is a desire of your heart — or if there are several desires of your heart — know that you are the one who is manifesting what you find in your life, and if you would change it, who else can do it for you? In Truth, only you — through the realization that you are more than the body, that you are more than the personality, that you are more than the limited focus of this space and time. Go first unto the Heart, beloved one, unto that quiet place of peace and of power, listening for the still small Voice which will reveal an idea, a feeling that you already have received, a balancing, a wholeness. For truly you are your Father's beloved Child. You are beauty incarnate. You are Love. You are free. You are free to be all that you desire to be: to express your total Self in its awakening.

# Seek Ye First

You are your Father's beloved Child in whom He is well pleased. Seek ye first the Kingdom of peace, and all else will be added unto you. Not added as the world would add, but revealed that you are already that which you would seek. My Kingdom — and yours — is not of the world. It is beyond and transcends the world. Can you take the world into the Kingdom? No. But you can — and will — take the Kingdom into the world, and it will transform the world.

Seek ye first the Kingdom.

# The Way Home

I desire to speak with you now about the way home, for you have asked and have decided at a very deep level to come Home, to come Home in this lifetime, to know in its fullness what Home is and Who Home is.

For Home is not a place afar off. Home is where you abide eternally. Home is the Love which you are. Home is the unconditional acceptance of the Love of the Heavenly Father and it is where you abide always, eternally.

What does Home feel like? It feels like the smile. It feels like the Love that comes forth from the heart. It feels as the compassion that you would extend unto another. It feels as the peace that abides with a deep breath, as one pauses for a moment and breathes in deeply of the Spirit. Home is where the heart is. You have heard that said.

There is much wisdom in the sayings of your world. All of the sayings of your world, if you will abide with them in silence and take them to their root source, have a great truth to share with you. Home is where the heart is. It is the Heart. It is the place of Love, the place where you connect again with the eternal being that you are: the holy Child — be it daughter or son — the holy Child of our Father, with Whom you are one, have always been and always will be, as you would see it. For you were created before time was, and after the purpose of time has been fulfilled, you will still be. Always.

You are the Heart of the Heavenly Father. You are the Light, the Energy which we have spoken of many times, the very Energy which gives you life and attracts the molecules of physicality in a particular design pattern so that you may express upon this plane. You are the very energy of Light. It can be measured even by your scientists in this day and time. There are many advances, as you would call it, in your scientific fields, which are becoming so exact that they are discovering what they call the reason for life, the basic life molecule, although it is smaller than a molecule and much more powerful.

You are living in an exciting time. And it is not that others are putting this on the platter before you. It is that you, yourself, are calling it forth because of your willingness to come Home, because you have asked at a very deep level to know Who you are. You have asked, "Who am I?" You have asked that throughout all of what you would see as lifetimes in varying degrees, and you have now made the decision and the commitment to know Who you are.

Know that you are the holy Child, and that all of your brothers and sisters are the holy Child as well. You are Love incarnate, walking about upon the face of our Holy Mother, the Earth, collecting unto yourself the molecules of physicality from the dust of our Holy Mother for what you would see as a time interval.

To do what? For what purpose? To extend the Love which you are. To extend it in many fashions: as you reach out and you take another's hand and you share with another the gentleness of the Love which they are, as you smile, as you say unto another one a word of support, as you share a shoulder with one who needs a shoulder for a moment or so to lean upon, as you open your heart to another and allow them to see that you know that it is safe to share who you are and you allow them to share who they are with you. And in the extension of Love, you experience yourSelf.

You are the Love of the Heavenly Father engaged in what you would see as a grand journey upon this plane at a specific time and place. You are the song of the Heavenly Father. You sing your song sometimes with joy, sometimes with questions. Always with the beauty that you are.

The way Home: is it afar off? Is it a place that you must first lay down the body before you find Home? No. Truly, it is not. Home is where you are in every moment when you choose to know the Love which you are, when you choose to have the courage to throw open the shutters of the Heart and to extend your very beingness unto another. That is where Home is. Home is where you are when you lift another in spirit — or in bodily form — to share the Love which you are with them.

Home is where the Heart is, and if you would know Home, pause and breathe in the golden white Light which surrounds you. Take it deeply into the very cells of the body and feel the peace that abides in the Heart. That peace is Home and it is instantly yours. You do not have to go through what you would see as many lifetimes of learning, of study and of rituals, of purifying yourself or even getting what is known in your time as the college degrees or the graduate degrees. For I will share with you: you have already graduated. You already have all wisdom, for nothing is hidden from you.

When you sit in your quiet times in the morning and you commune with me and with the Heavenly Father, ask whatever you would ask and it will be revealed unto you. There is nothing hidden from the desire of the Heart. It will always be revealed for you. It cannot be held from you except by your belief that you would hold it at arm's distance somewhere, and yet, if it is at arm's distance, you are touching it and you are not separate from it.

You are the delight of the Father, in whom He is well pleased. That is what Home feels like. Many of your brothers and sisters are calling out to know, "Where is Home? What does Home feel like?" Have you ever felt homesick? Homesick for a home that you have known, a physical home upon this plane? Have you ever traveled a journey and felt homesick and wanted to come home again? Yes.

And have you ever felt homesick for a home that you could not quite identify, and yet in the depth of your heart you felt so homesick because you knew there is a Home where your Heavenly Father awaits you? I would share with you, you have never left Home. You are loved with an everlasting Love, because you are that Love. You are Loved with an everlasting Love that is your Home.

Whenever you would come Home, pause in the midst of whatever you would see going on. Even if it be on one of your busy street corners, you can come Home. Pause and breathe. One deep breath, the simplicity of one deep breath affords you the opportunity of knowing you are Home.

Then you have the choice of going out again and forgetting — and you have done that many times. But you also know where to find Home. You know the address. You can pause in the midst of anything that is transpiring and remember the Love. That is Home.

Share that experience with your brothers and sisters who so desire to know, "Is there a Home? Where is Home? What does it feel like?" They will ask you to, "Take me home. Take me with you." And it is not that you will pick them up and transport them somewhere, but you will allow them to connect with the Home which they are.

Know you that many of the homeless, that you are seeing more and more in your consciousness, are symbolizing the search of mankind for Home? They are outpicturing for you the very search that the holy Child is upon to come Home again. And I will share with you that some of the homeless are more at Home than the ones who have a roof over their head, for they have truly learned that, "I and the Father are one," and that it does not matter what material possessions there are, that one can go in a freedom of Love, without having all of the trappings of the material possessions. Home is where the Heart is, and if the physical home be a cardboard box and the one living in the cardboard box knows himself/herself to be the Son/Daughter of our Father, that one will be Home.

You have been, beloved one, as the Prodigal Son, who went upon a far journey, seemingly, and thought himself to be far from the Kingdom of our Heavenly Father, far from Home. For, as you have experienced many journeys, many adventures, many lifetimes, many memories, there arises the feeling that, "If I have experienced so much and journeyed so far, I must have traveled far from my Father's kingdom." This has been the thought of the holy Child who desired to experience his/her infinite creativity, and, in the experiencing, found himself/herself to be mesmerized by the creations and thought himself/herself to be far away. And yet, you cannot be far from the Kingdom because the Kingdom is within you. You carry it with you, as you, always.

That is the great secret which is not hidden. The great secret is that you, in the peace and the Love and the joy and the compassion that you would extend unto another, you are the Kingdom. The Kingdom is not some geographical place that would be on star 97 in the galaxy of XYZ. It is not afar off. The Kingdom happens every moment when you smile, when you allow the chains upon the mind and Heart to be dissolved in the sunshine of your smile. It is simplicity itself.

There are many who will come and share with you wonderful techniques for finding your way Home, for finding the Kingdom. And these are all well and good, for they speak a language that ones want to hear, a language that often you have asked to hear, either in this lifetime or other lifetimes. And all of these techniques, workshops, methods have value in being a catalyst for remembrance, for there is no wisdom outside of you. It is not that you would go and take down a book from a shelf and it will instantly transform you, but it will be as a catalyst that will open the heart to the wisdom which you are, and you come Home in remembrance because you have never been away from Home except in your belief that you must be far from Home.

# The Way Home

The way Home is a journey without distance, for you are already there. It takes only your choice, your willingness to choose to be the peace and the Love which you are. It is that simple, although many would teach you that it is difficult and that you must do many things to find it.

You are already the Love of the Heavenly Father. You are already the sunshine, the great ray of Light, the one creation of your Father. Take that Truth deeply within. Ponder, meditate, abide with it, for there is but a percentage of you that is focused upon this time and this place, and much more of you is experiencing and expressing upon other planes and other realms. Even as you read this, your Spirit is soaring in other realms, very much in conversation with others that you would see as your brothers and sisters, others that express with different forms and beyond form. That is your unlimited Self. And as you catch a glimpse, you feel yourself transported far beyond what is happening just here in this lifetime, as it would be. And if you will pause and return again unto the place of the Heart and behold your unlimited Self, the events that go on in your day to day life, the relationships, the place of employment, even the traffic on your highways, will not seem to be such a big deal as they appear to be sometimes.

The way Home is through the Heart, abiding in stillness and in peace. The way Home is in extending Love, allowing the very shutters of the heart, that have been so tightly closed for what you would see as lifetimes, to be thrown wide open and to share with whoever stands in front of you the Love which you are, the joy which you are, the in-sights that you have gained, the insights which come from the inner wisdom.

The way Home is through relationships, for relationships will bring up in wonderful clarity whatever issues need to be healed. Not that they need a magic wand from without to do something to heal them and make them whole, but to look upon them with new eyes and to see them as already whole. To see the one who stands in front of you as the holy Child of our Father, the same as you, and to know that that one stands in front of you, in whatever behavior they are giving you, as a messenger for whatever you need to see anew. That is all they are there for. They are your servant. Believe it or not. Even if you would want to banish them and say, "Get out of my life forever," they are your servant and you have called them forth. You have asked them to bring you something you wish to heal, something you wish to know in its wholeness — even if they are pushing the biggest buttons you can imagine.

That is why you manifest for yourself the seeming individualities of the expression of the Heavenly Father: to know the great joy of being in relationship, of being able to relate to one another. And yes, once in a while to have issues that would come up to look at and to look beyond.

You have experienced ones that would come and stand before you and would say something that triggered an instant response within you — probably disproportionate to what actually was occurring. And you would ask yourself, when you came down from wherever you had gone — another planet perhaps — "Why am I feeling such emotion? Why am I feeling such energy about this? What does it bring up in me?" And as you abide with those questions, you will see perhaps what would look like a movie that will come before you, what will be as previous experiences, either in this lifetime or others. You will see how you have perceived hurt before. How you have feared before. How you have looked upon the very same circumstance other times and you have felt at such a loss. And yet this time you will look with new eyes, for you will see that you are no longer in the space that you were in, in what would be seen as a previous time or previous lifetimes. You are at a place where you can look upon what is happening and behold it anew.

You are your Father's holy Child. You are beautiful, and you have manifested for yourself all of the experiences for the very purpose of coming Home again. That is what is in process upon this plane. All of you, as seeming individuals, all of you as the One expressing as the many, are coming Home again. You are on the march, very much on the march. You have felt a nudging, a prodding in the last few months of your timing. You have felt that if you wanted to stand still, the very energies of whatever was going on around you would take you as a wave takes the pebble and carries it along in its motion. You are on the march, and it is not because some wave outside of you, some great master, some angel, some other entity or intelligence is doing it to you. It is because you have chosen to come Home and you have said, "Enough already with the delay. I am ready. Let whatever stands in front of me come up so I may look at it and I may see through it, for it is nothing but a veil." Everything that comes before you is as your messenger and is as thin as a veil, and you can see through it with holy vision.

Sometimes the veil has felt like a woolen blanket or even a lead curtain, perhaps. It becomes, now, a veil which parts easily.

You manifest relationship in your life so that you can know your oneness when a relationship is seemingly finished. A relationship is never truly ended for there is never a separation or a severing of a relationship. The Love which you are goes on forever, and what you have shared with another can never be taken away. The Love which you are is eternal. When one lays down the body, the form of communication with that one must change; that is all. It is no longer AT&T or MCI or Sprint that handles the call. You develop a new phone company, and you phone Home.

When one of your brothers or sisters with whom you have shared much desires to take their form to another geographical location perhaps, and to be companion to someone else, you allow your Love to go before them, making the pathway smooth, and you say, "Okay, Father, send me the next one to love!" And He does.

The way Home is through the Heart, through the Heart which you are allowing to open, allowing to be as the master. The mind is the servant of the Heart. It is not the other way around, although your world would teach you that the mind comes first and must rule the heart. You have heard that said many times: "Do not be foolish. Do not let your heart lead you. Use your head." In Truth it is the other way around. The Truth of your Reality, the Truth of your being, is that you are Love and that you can never be hurt except in your belief.

As you desire to know, in conscious awareness, the nature of Home, pause and breathe. Abiding in that peace, at some point you will feel a stirring, an activation, which signals the *dynamic* quality of Home, an uplifting of the very soul in joy.

Many of you find yourselves sitting before the machines, the computers and other machines, during your daytime, spending many hours in front of mechanical means, doing very little with the body. And as you desire to know the dynamic quality of Home, you may want to do some physical activity of getting out and running with the bare feet in the meadow. How long has it been since you ran in the meadow with bare feet?

Or with the bare feet upon the sand?

The Way Home

If you would feel the dynamic quality of Home, take yourself out of doors. Take off the shoes. Allow yourself to be unconstricted, and feel the energy of the Holy Mother. Run with the wind. Run in grand freedom and shout. Shout to the Heavens your very being. You are God expressing upon this plane in very dynamic quality. That is Who you are. That is the way Home.

Returning Home does not have to be done in what you would see as a certain ritual, sitting in a certain posture for a required length of time, becoming very spiritual. For you are already spiritual. It is Who you are from before time began. Allow yourself to express.

Do you know why I enjoy being amongst you in the expression afforded by my beloved friend and teacher, the one known as Judith? Do you know why I embrace you, why I touch you on the shoulder, why I ruffle the hair? It is to be in communion with the Energy which you are. The very hair itself is Love in tangible form, the same as the arm, the same as the shoulder. I come and I touch to allow the vibrations to be shared. That is why you enjoy the hugs with each other. There is much that goes on with the hug. It says unto another person, "Yes, I welcome you into my Heart," for that is where you take one in a hug. You take them to your Heart. You say, "Yes, I have the courage to be open and vulnerable with you. I will take you in and I will share with you Who I am. I will share with you the very Energy that you are and that I am in physical form."

Whenever you want to connect with Home, reach out and touch another one in a hug, hold a hand, caress a loved one's face. That is what Home feels like. The smile. The beautiful smile. The smile of two friends who are one.

And as you allow yourself to express, you allow the body to be the balance which it is designed to be. As you allow yourself the freedom of coming Home in each moment and knowing the freedom at a very dynamic level, you allow the very cells of the body to do what they are designed to do: to express the Light of Consciousness. And as you allow the cells of the body to be and to radiate the Light, do you know what happens? Even more radiance, more of the Energy is allowed to course through the molecules of physicality until... until what, beloved one?

Until there is the actual physical ascension where the cells of the body are so light that they cannot be held upon this plane and you will see yourself ascending. All of you who desire to ascend the body will experience that in this lifetime. Some of you have already experienced that in your times of meditation, your times of joy, where you felt yourself to be lifting up. Now, it does not mean that you have ascended the body to the Heavens and you do not come back again, but you have felt yourself to be so light, you have felt a change, a change that actually could be and was registered in the body. You have felt yourself ascending.

For as you ascend in consciousness, in the awareness of the Light which you are, of the joy which you are, you allow the very cells of the body to become lighter. It has been your belief system, so tightly held throughout what you would see as many lifetimes, which has said unto you that you are heavy, physical, dense matter that must be held upon this plane by a certain attraction called gravity.

Many of you, when you have heard what is known as music, be it upon an instrument or be it through the voice of a friend, or your own voice, have felt yourself transported somewhere. And you *have* been transported somewhere. You have been taken out of the very narrow focus of what you have seen your world to be and you have allowed yourself to open the shutters of the heart, the blinders that would be upon the eyes, and to see with a more expanded vision, to feel with a more expanded feeling, the Heart of yourSelf. And as you allow your Self to express, you bring forth the power of Who you are. Many of you have manifested for yourself lifetimes when it was not safe to express, when it was not safe to speak, to sing, to share your Truth, and you have come to this life experience with a memory that is deeply embedded even within what you would see as the cells of the body that it is not safe to speak a view that perhaps differs from your brother's. It is not safe, acceptable to sing, to be joyous, spontaneous. And many of you have reinforced that belief with your own upbringing, your childhood as you have known it.

I share with you now a new image: you are the holy Child of the Heavenly Father and it is safe — not only safe but it is imperative — to express Who you are, to shout it to the very Heavens, to whisper it to the grass, to know your oneness with all of creation. Home feels like joy. Home feels like wholeness. Home feels like acceptance. Home feels like Love. Home feels like peace. Home feels like the smile. Home feels like the embrace of a friend. Home feels like the word which is offered in support. Home feels like the home that is opened — the physical home — to one who needs a bed for that night, a meal, warm clothing. Home feels like Love itself.

Each of you as you read these words can go deep within yourself, within the Heart, and you can connect with a quality that you can extend unto another: something that you may have practiced, something that you may have always known, something that you feel at home with. You have beautiful gifts to share with others. And in this lifetime you have chosen various ones to hone, to develop. In other lifetimes you have chosen other qualities to work with, to experience. That is why you need never envy anyone what you would see as their ability to do something, for you in another lifetime have honed that very quality yourself — otherwise, you would not admire what they are doing. You would have no point of relatedness to understand and to appreciate what they are doing. You would not know how to value it if you had not already experienced it yourself.

You can sit and watch someone, and you can feel yourself for a moment to be that one. You can feel yourself to be in their shoes, their sandals, their ice skates, their ballet slippers. You can feel yourself to be one with them. In that moment you are experiencing what you perceive them to be doing — and in your consciousness you are participating with them, you as the supportive, integrative Light which you are.

So you need never sit in envy of anyone for what you would see as their qualities and talents and abilities. You have already done it, and you are working on qualities that probably someone else envies you for. It is the way of the world.

In my Father's house are many mansions. Many that you will experience. Many that you have experienced, as you see time to be. In my Father's house there are many planes of expression.

You are Home. You have always been Home. As the creative Child, there were qualities that you yet wanted to experience. You wanted to experience how it felt to be a mother, a father. How it felt to be in relationship. How it felt to be a great warrior. How it felt to be the servant. How it felt to be driving one of your great semi-trucks. And how else would you know what it felt like except to come and to do it? You are the holy Child, Who has desired to experience infinite creativity.

Home is not a far off place that would be defined as Heaven, that you have to lay down the body to go unto, and if you've been good enough, Saint Peter might let you in. Home is where you are each time you pause and you breathe and you say, "Thank you, Father. I am home." It is simplicity itself. It is Love and it is dynamic.

Let no one tell you that Home has to be a place where you sit and twiddle the thumbs or, with wings on the back, you play your harp. Not everyone, I suppose, likes harp music.

If you would know Home, breathe. Come unto the place of the Heart and abide in the Heart. Call on me, for I am always Home.

You are the Light of the world. You have chosen to express with the molecules of physicality upon this plane at this time for the very purpose of coming Home in conscious awareness — not only for what you would see as yourself, but also for your brothers and sisters: yourSelf.

Breathe with me right now, breathe in the golden white Light which you are. For this is truly Who you are. You are a golden white ray of Light, the Energy of Light. Breathe in the golden white Light which you are and take it deeply within the cells of the body. Feel it energizing every cell in the body.

Breathe again, and connect with Home. You are Home, beloved one.

Welcome home.

So be it.

Oakbridge University Press

Publishers of metaphysical books and materials.

The books that we publish reflect our desire to support
and encourage the emerging consciousness of Light and
Love, and to assist the awakening of all humanity in Oneness.

# Jeshua: The Personal Christ Volume II

Channeled information from Jeshua ben Joseph. Jesus talks about Meditation, The Descent into Matter, Falling in Love, Ascending in Love, The Days to Come, Manifesting, The Age of Enlightenment, Ascension, Prayer and much more. Foreword by Alan Cohen.

*There is nothing a human can do on this planet that is more spectacular than to examine the piece of god that resides in themselves. The loving Jeshua material is uplifting and powerful. This really is necessary reading in this new age!*
— Lee Carroll - Channel for Kryon

208 pages, paperback   $12.95
ISBN 1-878555-09-X

Beloved and holy Child of our Father, when first you thought to be upon what you now call our holy Mother, the Earth, you came as the Light being that you are. You came with the creativity of the holy Child to see, "What more can I create?"

For, verily, before time began, you, as the Child of the Creator, flexed your figurative creative wings, and as one great Thought to experience the beauty of energy in form, you imagined, put the images into action, and brought forth energy into form.

Now, the Thought energy did not coalesce right away, for there would be — although this was just the beginning of what you have called time — eons of time before the form would come into what you now recognize and know. The Earth, the planets, the universes were/are very much a Light energy and you were/are Light energy, and the forms that you brought forth were nebulous, cloud-like. You knew yourself to be Light, and the creations were Light. You were very much one with what you *are* creating — for truly, it is not an event that has happened a long time ago; it is what is happening moment by moment as the Light and the Consciousness that you are.

And as the Earth came into being, you thought to create upon and out of the substance of Earth. You thought to bring together frequencies and vibrations of the Light into various combinations to see what would result. And with those thoughts were born the clouds, the energies of the oceans, of the rivers, of the streams, and the more dense material known as the mountains and the hills in their various formations.

In due time, you thought to experience life upon this plane, and you came as the Light being that you are. Not with the attraction of the molecules of physicality that you see yourself now surrounded by... but you came as the Light being to experience, "What would it feel like to be upon what I have created?" ...

... Chapter 4 **"You've Gone As Far As You Can Go"**

# Jeshua: The Personal Christ
## Volume III
# Don't Look For Me In a Tortilla Chip

In this volume, Jeshua/Jesus explains the Bible in terms we can understand today. Passages such as The Ten Commandments, The Sermon on the Mount and The Beatitudes, Isaiah 40 (Comfort Ye My People) take on new and expanded meaning, and in a very personal way Jeshua/Jesus describes choosing His disciples, His baptism, His temptations and beginning His ministry. Everyone who wants to know Him better and to understand the writings of the Scriptures more fully will want to have this volume at their desk and bedside table.

Includes a special cameo chapter: Mother Mary talks about Holy Communion.

*This is the time that the Christ Consciousness is revealing itself in many ways, blessing us with the wisdom we need to step into our own mastery and enlightenment. Judith Coates has listened to the 'still quiet voice' within, and in doing so has opened for us all the grace that lies within us all.*
— James F. Twyman

182 pages,   paperback   $12.95
ISBN 1-878555-12-X

Child of our Father, there was a time in which I spoke unto you what has come to be known as The Sermon on the Mount. The Mount was a high place, a hill upon which we gathered so that the multitudes could be seated all around, for by this time many knew of the healings which had taken place and were anxious to learn of what I would teach.

First, a word about the Scriptures which you have now. Know you that what you have recorded in your Holy Bible as to my teachings are someone's notes of what they remembered me saying. The words which you have extant in your Scriptures today, the words ascribed to me, are a compilation of remembrances, cryptic messages often preserved by oral tradition, handed down from one person to another. These messages were originally based on someone's summation of what they heard me teach, similar to the notes you have taken at some of your workshops and lectures.

Further, know you that as your Scriptures have been handed down to you, seemingly by others and yet it has been an evolution in which you have participated, the translations which have been made and the words which have been chosen have often taken on different meanings than that which was originally intended. For example:

*Blessed are the poor in spirit....* Now, I did not say *poor* in spirit. The word which I used meant simple, uncomplicated, un-complex. Blessed are the simple in spirit. Blessed are the ones who know their simplicity — not their complexity — having no focus upon a world of shoulds and schedules and judgments. *For their's is the Kingdom of Heaven,* as they abide in the realm of uncomplicatedness....

...Chapter 2 **"The Beatitudes"**

# Jesus and Mastership

## The Gospel According to Jesus of Nazareth

Jesus tells His story in His own words. Dictated through the Rev. James C. Morgan, Unity minister, this is the day to day account of Jesus' life from age 18, when He went to India to study, through the crucifixion and resurrection. He tells of choosing His disciples, His relationship with Miriam, His ministry and why He taught what He did. Now in its third printing. A best-seller, nationwide. A new Bible.

390 pages, indexed, paperback    $14.95
ISBN 1-878555-00-6

## A Message from Jesus of Nazareth to You, the Reader:

I feel the account of my life on the earth plane about 2,000 years ago, given in this manner, will have more meaning and be more accurate than the messages I have inspired others to write. They were excellent channels, but this is a better way. Naturally, the language we are using is the current idiom rather than a translation of the Aramaic I spoke long ago. There will be no conjecture or supposing. It must be perfectly clear to anyone who reads this book that my sole purpose in living and giving of myself was to awaken man to his true potential.

The people of that time were living in a state of mind that was quite similar to the state of mind of most people today. There were the rich and the poor, the well and the sick, those who worshipped many gods, those who worshipped one God, and those who worshipped none or self. Men were the rulers and women their chattel. There were the cruel and the gentle. There were those who hated and those who loved. Crime was rampant, and seemingly might ruled. Yes, it was much the same as today— there was happiness and there was sadness. There was much that was good and there was that which was not so good. At that, it was a good world for mankind in which to learn and grow.

This is only a very meager description of the kind of world into which I incarnated. I returned to the earth plane with an intense desire to help man raise himself to a better life and to realize his own vast and unlimited spiritual powers. These powers were being used incorrectly and thus bringing undesirable conditions forth into the lives of a large portion of mankind.

I believed that I should stir the people up to awaken them to their own spiritual self just as I had found mine. So this is the reason I took the action that I did. I knew it would create commotion and call attention to what I was teaching.

Mankind must know the truth and not someone's interpretation of what I said or meant. It is time for all men to make ready for the new age coming by the year 2,000. Only those who accept the living God as their creator and saviour will survive the worldwide tribulations that are coming. Those who grow spiritually will reach the heights of glory in God's kingdom of peace and happiness. All others will be in turmoil and pain of their own choosing....

...Introductory *Message*

## Return Passage
## Journey of the Soul

### Michael Harvey

An engrossing novel of reincarnation: lifetimes of power, passion and intrigue, in Atlantis, Galilee, etc., culminating with a modern day incarnation which illumines all lifetimes. The final chapter will surprise you with a beautiful twist of an ending.

Have you ever tried to explain reincarnation to someone? This book does it easily.

*This book is beautifully written, very empowering and inspirational. After reading it, you will have no choice but to deeply honor the path you are on and love yourself and everyone in your life a little more. Highly recommended!*
— Bookstore, Seattle, Washington

232 pages, paperback $12.95
ISBN 1-878555-02-2

The first report came from Mu. A huge earthquake of 9.6 magnitude had devastated islands to the north. The casualties were enormous. Air and sea rescue units were being mobilized to assist survivors. Mu itself was bracing for a gigantic tidal wave. We looked in horror as the extent of the damage became apparent. The few survivors interviewed told of horrendous loss of life and property.

The following morning newscasts centered on rescue attempts and the magnitude of damage. So far, the expected tidal wave hadn't materialized. The first newscast received in space was a rehash of news I'd seen earlier. I was ready to turn off the set when the program was interrupted by an important news flash. Another devastating quake had ripped the southern Pole. Again the quake was of unprecedented magnitude. It was so strong the recorder was unable to measure the intensity. If this were indeed true and not a malfunction of the recording equipment, nothing could have withstood the quake.

Still glued to the television monitor, my mind drifted to my stupidity a couple of days ago. What had possessed me to succumb to such irrational emotions? Sinta had asked to speak to me with such urgency I couldn't refuse her. Normally drones only reply when spoken to, but again she displayed the animation I'd witnessed when she'd related her faith in a Creator.

I led her out of earshot of the household as a citizen didn't talk to a drone unless it was to give instructions. Again I noticed the astounding fact of an intensity and intelligence shining in the blueness of her eyes.

"Please," she implored, "take me to Master Noah. The time has arrived." What was she talking about, what lunacy was Noah involved in? How on earth had he contacted her? "What are you talking about, Sinta?" She took my hand in hers (again an action no drone was permitted) and without hesitation explained her request.

"Noah," she said, "is calling all true believers. I can hear him distinctly in my head. All The Ones now have this ability." Flabbergasted, I demanded to know if she now considered herself a member of The Ones, who, to my knowledge were all human and certainly not drones. "Oh, yes," she replied....

...Chapter 15

Yes, I would like to order the following books:
Please send (quantity)

| | | |
|---|---|---|
| ___ | Jeshua: The Personal Christ I | $12.95 |
| ___ | Jeshua: The Personal Christ II | $12.95 |
| ___ | Jeshua: The Personal Christ III | $12.95 |
| ___ | Jesus and Mastership | $14.95 |
| ___ | Return Passage | $12.95 |

Please include postage: $3.50 for the 1st book
 plus 50 cents for each additional book.

Enclosed is $_____

Name _____

Address _____

City _____ State ____ Zip ____

Telephone _____
Visa/MasterCard information:

Account #_____
Expiration Date ____ | ____
Signature _____

**Oakbridge University Press**
**4007 Harbor Ridge N.E.**
**Tacoma, WA 98422**
**(253) 952-3285**
**E-mail: Judith@Oakbridge.org**
**www.Oakbridge.org**

Yes, I would like to order the following books:
Please send (quantity)

____ Jeshua: The Personal Christ I                    $12.95

____ Jeshua: The Personal Christ II                   $12.95

____ Jeshua: The Personal Christ III                  $12.95

____ Jesus and Mastership                             $14.95

____ Return Passage                                   $12.95


Please include postage: $3.50 for the 1st book
plus 50 cents for each additional book.

Enclosed is $_____

Name _____

Address _____

City _____ State ____ Zip _____

Telephone _____
Visa/MasterCard information:

Account #_____
Expiration Date ____ | ____
Signature _____

**Oakbridge University Press**
**4007 Harbor Ridge N.E.**
**Tacoma, WA 98422**
**(253) 952-3285**
**E-mail: Judith@Oakbridge.org**
**www.Oakbridge.org**

Yes, I would like to order the following books:
Please send (quantity)

____ Jeshua: The Personal Christ I                    $12.95

____ Jeshua: The Personal Christ II                   $12.95

____ Jeshua: The Personal Christ III                  $12.95

____ Jesus and Mastership                             $14.95

____ Return Passage                                   $12.95


Please include postage: $3.50 for the 1st book
  plus 50 cents for each additional book.

Enclosed is $_____

Name _____

Address _____

City _____ State ____ Zip _____

Telephone _____
Visa/MasterCard information:

Account #_____
Expiration Date ____ | ____
Signature _____

**Oakbridge University Press**
**4007 Harbor Ridge N.E.**
**Tacoma, WA 98422**
**(253) 952-3285**
**E-mail: Judith@Oakbridge.org**
**www.Oakbridge.org**

Yes, I would like to order the following books:
Please send (quantity)

| | | |
|---|---|---|
| ___ | Jeshua: The Personal Christ I | $12.95 |
| ___ | Jeshua: The Personal Christ II | $12.95 |
| ___ | Jeshua: The Personal Christ III | $12.95 |
| ___ | Jesus and Mastership | $14.95 |
| ___ | Return Passage | $12.95 |

Please include postage: $3.50 for the 1st book
 plus 50 cents for each additional book.

Enclosed is $_____

Name _____

Address _____

City _____ State ____ Zip _____

Telephone _____
Visa/MasterCard information:

Account #_____
Expiration Date ____ | ____
Signature _____

**Oakbridge University Press**
**4007 Harbor Ridge  N.E.**
**Tacoma, WA 98422**
**(253) 952-3285**
**E-mail: Judith@Oakbridge.org**
**www.Oakbridge.org**